The Art of Storytelling
for Teachers and Pupils

The Art of Storytelling for Teachers and Pupils

Using Stories to Develop Literacy in Primary Classrooms

Elizabeth Grugeon and Paul Gardner

With contributions from members of the Primary Team in
The School of Education, De Montfort University, Bedford:

Georgina Elton
Paul Frecknall
Lorraine Hubbard
Nick Hubbard
Marilyn Leask
Barbara Leedham
John Sampson
Carol Smith (Portfields Combined School, Milton Keynes)

David Fulton Publishers
London

David Fulton Publishers Ltd
Ormond House, 26–27 Boswell Street, London WC1N 3JD

First published in Great Britain by David Fulton Publishers 2000

Note: The rights of Elizabeth Grugeon and Paul Gardner to be identified
as the authors of this work has been asserted by them in accordance
with the Copyright, Designs and Patents Act 1988.

Copyright © Elizabeth Grugeon and Paul Gardner 2000

British Library Cataloguing in Publication Data
A catalogue record for this book is available from the British Library

ISBN 1–85346–617–4

Typeset by Elite Typesetting Techniques, Eastleigh, Hampshire
Printed in Great Britain by The Cromwell Press Ltd, Trowbridge, Wilts.

Contents

Acknowledgements

The authors would like to thank students and colleagues with whom they have worked at De Montfort University, Bedford for providing examples of their own and children's work. In particular, they would like to thank the following individuals and institutions for their help and permission to use examples from practice:

Sue Collins; Sarah Cumming; Emma Lazenby; Belinda Louch; Vicky Mansell; Wendy Quince; Vikki Slater; Kathryn Stone; Jane Templeman; Manjula Koria, Raising Expectations and Achievement in Learning Project, Milton Keynes; Rashida Kazi, Diana Cornell, Parminder Jolly and Bilingual Classroom Assistants, Raising Expectations and Achievement in Learning Project, Buckinghamshire.

Bushfield Middle School

Portfields Combined School

Shepherdswell First School

Wyvern First School - all in Milton Keynes.

In case of failure to obtain permission to include copyright material in this book the authors and publishers apologise and undertake to make good omissions in subsequent printings.

Thanks to David Grugeon for his help and advice.

Introduction

Storytelling and literacy

At the start of the new millennium the definition of literacy has taken on multiple electronic possibilities. But this is a book about the foundations of literacy in orality, in the words, stories and culture of every individual. In her book *On Being Literate*, Margaret Meek describes how young children move into literacy when they discover 'what the story is: the move from words into sentences', when they begin to recognise writing and reading (Meek 1991:102) but she adds that before that move is possible they must learn to *tell* the story. She makes a special case for the relation of stories and storytelling to literacy.

> ... storytelling is a universal habit, as part of our common humanity. As far as we know all cultures have forms of narrative. Stories are part of our conversations, our recollections, our plans, our hopes, our fears. Young and old, we all tell stories as soon as we begin to explain or describe events and actions, feelings and motives ...
>
> From the stories we hear as children we inherit the ways in which we talk about how we feel, the values which we hold to be important, and what we regard as the truth. We discover in stories ways of saying and telling that let us know who we are. So before they even attempt the first stages of literacy, children have heard and told many stories ...
>
> If we are to understand the relation of storytelling to literacy, we must see the value and nature of narrative as a means by which human beings everywhere, represent and structure their world.
>
> (Meek 1991:103)

This book explores the relation of storytelling to literacy and the role of story in human life: we hear the voices of many contributors telling about their understanding and experience of storytelling; the experts who have written some of the important recent texts about storytelling; our colleagues at De Montfort University who look at story from a variety of subject disciplines; teachers, children and families from different communities and cultures and most importantly, the voices of teachers and trainees who are working in schools with the children whose voices are the main focus of our concern.

The book is in three parts. The first three chapters, written by Elizabeth Grugeon, discuss the value and enjoyment of oral storytelling in school and are based on experience of working with teachers, students and children for a number of years. The second part has been compiled by Paul Gardner and reflects the response of a number of our colleagues in teacher education to the role of story in their different disciplines. The third part, again written by Paul Gardner, deals with the social dimension of story; the function of story as a means of reflecting and articulating social identity in the context of our everyday life.

Chapter 1, 'Oral storytelling', looks at the school as a context for storytelling and the role of the teacher as a storyteller. It considers children's spontaneous and informal storytelling, the role of story in children's personal growth and development and in their confident acquisition of skills required for literate competence.

Chapter 2, 'Reading about storytelling', is an overview of some of the key texts about storytelling in school that the teachers might find a useful resource. It provides a theoretical rationale for anyone wishing to embark on acquiring the art of storytelling and supplies a wide range of practical ideas.

Chapter 3, 'Teachers and pupils learn the art of storytelling', draws on many examples of teachers working with children – some experienced practitioners, some novices. As they demonstrate and reflect upon their practice, we learn about successful strategies for the use of stories across the primary age range and the value of these activities and approaches for both teacher and taught.

Chapter 4, 'Story across the curriculum', is a selective dip into some of the ways teachers have used story to enhance primary practice. The examples provide possible models which may be adapted to suit particular curriculum demands.

Chapter 5, 'Narrative, school and community', develops the theme of the relationship between story and the lived experience of children and their families. Storytelling and the construction of stories are seen to be social events capable of cementing human relationships in both the classroom and the wider community.

Chapter 6, 'Language, story and identity', draws upon the experiences of bilingual children and adults. It considers language as symbol of social identity and suggests ways in which bilingual storytelling might be incorporated into the classroom.

In the postscript, we offer readers an original story, rooted in the multilingual context that is typical of an increasing number of classrooms in modern Britain.

Is there a future for the oral story?

As the new millennium starts, it might seem that the oral tradition of storytelling has been superseded by electronic media or that it has been pushed out of the way by a rather narrow definition of schooled literacy. We might ask nervously where in the National Literacy Framework is there space for telling stories if targets are to be met. This book will suggest that there is not only time and space but that storytelling has a role to play in development of literacy for children at all stages of the primary curriculum. A teacher reaffirms this.

Storytelling in Year 6. Is it still possible?

Carol Smith, Portfields Combined School, Milton Keynes

In the midst of national target setting, LEA target setting, booster classes' SATS tests, SATS practise tests, head teachers' expectations, parental expectations and the Literacy Hour, is there any room left for the simple art of storytelling? If there is, and surely there must be, how does it squeeze into a packed curriculum? Does it really matter? By Year 6, surely the children don't need to be told or to tell stories any more? They just need to do lots of textual analysis, lots of grammatical awareness and lots of reading – group, shared, paired, guided, independent … Or do they? Is that enough?

Having worked with Year 6 for several years and been part of an increasing pressure on the children to do well in their SATS and the drive to raise standards, it has been a privilege to have been part of the year group's achievement of exceeding the Secretary of State for Education's National Target in English in 1999, three years ahead of schedule. I do not know how to stop children telling stories or how to teach without storytelling being an intrinsic part of good English teaching …

Is it difficult to arouse the children's interest in stories? No, not at all. Each year group spends one term on a storytelling theme, as well as a constant appreciation of the children's own stories, so by Year 6 the children have been immersed in stories. The interest in stories begins

Τηε Ανχιεντ Γρεεκσ
Ψεαρ 6 Ηολιδαψ Ηομεωορκ
Γρεεκ Μψτησ ανδ Λεγενδσ
Ωελχομε!

When you become a member of Year 6 in September, our first work in English and History will be about the history, culture and stories of ancient Greece.

During the holiday we would like you to read and find out a little about ancient Greek myths and legends. You may know a few already, such as the sad story of Daedalus and Icarus who dared to fly too near to the sun or the heroic Twelve Labours of Herakles or poor Persephone, punished so cruelly for eating just a few pomegranate seeds. You may have to do some research in the library or ask your family what Greek myths they know.

Try to think of an interesting way to retell and present your myth to your class when you return to school in September ~ it could be as a story board, as a short puppet play or even remembered and told as if *you* were one of the 'heroes' in your chosen myth. Try to have your version ready to bring to school on Tuesday 7 September. Be prepared to share your work!

Ηαππψ Ηολιδαψ!

Ανχιεντ Γρεεκσ 1
Θυλψ 1999
Πεγγψ Αλλιν
Χαρολ Σμιτη
Χατηψ Πεττιπιεχε

in Reception and the Early Years Unit. 'Stories from around the World' moves through a story-rich curriculum to 'Telling Tales' in Year 4 – a close look at Fairy Tales and their particular ingredients. In Year 6, the Autumn term has a Greek focus and the children are able to make connections to other myths and legends studied in Year 3 and their similarities with fairy tales. Their understanding and appreciation of the need for 'heroes' in storytelling gives them an insight into common themes in a broad range of storytelling devices. Robin Hood is instantly comparable with Perseus, Theseus, Odysseus, Herakles and modern 'super' heroes such as James Bond, Superman, Batman and Grant Mitchell from EastEnders. We were all convinced that the script writers were well versed in their knowledge of Greek mythology at the time of Tiffany's death; the connections between Herakles' tragic personal life and Grant Mitchell's were spotted by the children before I could point it out. Comparisons were made between the tragic life of Tiffany in *EastEnders*, Marion in *Robin of Sherwood* (Morpurgo 1999) and King Minos' daughter in Theseus and the Minotaur. Studying Ancient Greece in Year 6, with all the wonderful myths and legends that enrich this period of history, gives such diversity to the children's understanding of how really good stories have been passed down over the centuries and have influenced and continue to influence writers. They influence the children's own stories when in Year 6 Spring term the children are encouraged to develop their own oral storytelling skills. Favourite stories are worked on in the Literacy Hour or English time and may develop into whole class or group stories.

Does this help children to become more literate, better writers and better readers, more confident in speaking aloud and more able to express their ideas clearly? Surely it must.

It is in the spirit of such optimism that this book has been written.

References

Meek, Margaret (1991) *On Being Literate*. London: Bodley Head.
Morpurgo, Michael (1999) *Robin of Sherwood*.

CHAPTER 1

Oral storytelling

Nervously, but well practiscd, I set out on my adventure as a storyteller. To my surprise, I thoroughly enjoyed my first experience. Amazed at the deep, attentive silence which reigned over this very boisterous class as I told the story, I felt that the experience had really captivated them. Using my whole body in its telling, my hands, face even my eyes could express the story. Without a book, I felt that I was able to use my voice more expressively, concentrating on each word. As I told the story I realised that its shape was the most important aspect to remember. The details were unique to that particular telling and would change each time I told the story. I was pleased when even the most inhibited children began to join in the repetition; the children had become totally absorbed in the words of the story and so had I. We really enjoyed the experience, a fact that I had observed with delight as I watched the expression on their faces.
(Sue Collins in Grugeon 1998:53)

Reading or telling?

Most of us, when faced with the option of reading aloud from a book or telling the same story without a book in our hands, would probably rather read it. Trainee teachers, faced with the challenge of telling a story to their class for the first time, often express trepidation; a student typically recalls, 'When story time arrived, I remember feeling quite anxious … what I was about to do was quite new to me.'

It is daunting to have to leave the safety and authority of a written page. Telling the story rather than reading it is an altogether different experience; there is no safety net when you forget what comes next, no pictures to support your telling, only your voice and your body language, only eye contact with your audience. You have to use your own words and be prepared to improvise, even though you may be telling a well-known tale and using words that are familiar to your listeners: 'I'll huff and I'll puff and I'll blow your house down'; 'Someone's been sleeping in my bed …'. The magic words 'Once upon a time …' will raise a myriad of possibilities for your expectant audience. Perhaps that is the difference between reading and telling; reading is a process of sharing and interpreting a text that someone else has produced but telling a story is a unique and personal performance. You are on your own when you tell a story and on that occasion, whatever the tale, wherever you first read it or heard it, it becomes your story, your version which you adapt to the needs of your audience. Perhaps Goldilocks wandered off into the woods on her own because her friend couldn't come to play, or Red Riding Hood got impatient while her mother chatted to a neighbour and she set off alone because she could not wait to show Granny her new coat. Telling sets you free from the written text and allows you to alter and add to the original version and to adapt it to the needs of your audience.

There is no need to be fearful; we are all much better at telling stories than we realise and we do it all the time. Consider what you will do when you put this book down; you will probably be involved in a social activity, talking to your friends or family; and the talk will almost certainly involve telling or hearing about some of the events of your, or their, day and as you or they tell about these events you will be shaping these happenings into a narrative, a story. You will edit and mould this to create the desired response in your audience, often using phrases like 'And you will never guess what happened next …', 'Who do you think came in then? …', 'I have never been so surprised in my life …'. We all use these phrases to create effect when we are telling stories about how we coped with the most mundane daily events. Telling stories to extricate ourselves from awkward predicaments is something we are all very good at. You probably know the ones about the car that had a puncture on the way to hand in an assignment to your tutor or the computer that crashed as the final full stop was being added to the report five minutes before the deadline. The children you teach are very adept at these too, possibly even more creative with the truth than we are!

When I assured a class of trainee teachers that they were all expert storytellers, one student was adamant that she never told stories. Her friend turned to her in amazement and asked what she had been doing on the way to the university that morning; she had apparently given a dramatic account of what she had done when she realised that the tuna she had put in her son's sandwiches was past its sell-by date. Gossip and storytelling are all part of a similar process and involve the same skills; exchanging gossip can involve elaborate storytelling.

I have become aware of this over a period of time from contact with a number of writers and storytellers: Margaret Meek, Jimmy Britton, Harold, Betty and Michael Rosen, Mary Medlicott, Tony Aylwin, Judith Graham, Carol Fox, Edie Garvie, Eve Gregory, Eileen Colwell, teachers taking part in the National Oracy Project, and most of all from the work I have shared with students at De Montfort University (formerly Bedford College Of Higher Education).

Acquiring a repertoire of stories

The stories that you may choose to tell in school will often be traditional tales: myths, legends, fables, folk and fairy tales which

> all reflect communal ways of making sense of experience … they offer alternative worlds which embody imaginative, emotional and spiritual truths about the universe and are a central resource for storytelling in education, particularly in multicultural classrooms. (Grainger 1997:23)

It is likely that everyone has a basic repertoire of what I would call nursery stories. Along with nursery rhymes and songs, these are the first stories we heard, in our homes and at school, when we were very young. Depending on our personal histories we may remember more or less of these and they may be monocultural and eurocentric or multicultural and world-wide. In some families, grandmothers still tell stories and make a link with an oral culture. One of my students, who had enjoyed the Punjabi stories that her grandmother had told her, wondered whether this trend was dying out. Talking to the children in her school, she was delighted to be able to track down stories from many parts of the Indian subcontinent as well as others from Cornwall and the Caribbean. These stories, passed down within families, are in danger of being lost along with many less well-known traditional tales from all over the world.

Teachers need to develop a repertoire of traditional tales that extends beyond the nursery and goes further than the mainly European collections that many of us have grown up with – largely fairy and folk tales which were first published in the seventeenth, eighteenth and nineteenth centuries by folklorists and collectors like the Grimm Brothers, Charles Perrault and Hans Andersen. At the end of the twentieth century they are most familiar to children in Walt Disney versions as books and videos. Telling stories from a wider cultural perspective can broaden this relatively narrow, Eurocentric experience and challenge gender, race and class stereotypes.

Learning to tell by telling

There are many excellent collections of stories from around the world and beautifully illustrated versions of single tales that we can use to extend our repertoire. However, the book often seems to exert powerful authority and it may seem difficult or pointless to attempt to retell a complex story that has been beautifully written and illustrated. In my experience, the most satisfying way to add to one's collection is by listening to stories being told. I have learnt some of my best stories by retelling those that I have heard a friend or colleague relating. Tony Aylwin taught me the story of Mr Waggle and Mr Woggle at a conference I attended some years ago and I have been passing on my version to students ever since. It's a very simple story that never fails to grip the youngest audience as the two protagonists keep failing to find each other at home; 'And Mr Waggle went up the hill and down the hill and up the hill and down the hill until he came to Mr Woggle's house. And he went 'pop' as he knocked on the door.' At another conference, Judith Graham introduced me to the African story, 'Bimwillie and the Zimwi'. I tell this one a lot and I keep a large pink and white shell in my room as a prop when I sing Bimwilli's song: 'I found a shell from out of the sea/A shell the big wave gave to me/ It's pink inside like the sunset sky/ When I listen I hear the big waves sigh.' This is a story that warns about the risk involved in letting your younger sibling out of your sight and the risks involved in talking to strangers. From Mary Medlicott I learnt a Korean tale that tells about the power and importance of stories and how we neglect them at our peril. There are many anecdotes about the arrival of stories in the world and I remember sitting at the back of a multicultural school hall in Bedford while Mrs Daniels, the deputy head, held the whole school spellbound as she told an Anansi tale about how the first stories came to be told. I learnt a version of 'The land where no one ever dies', from listening to Betty Rosen. This is a powerful tale which I have told many times and never failed to startle my listeners, particularly the person sitting next to me, when I suddenly grab their arm with the words, 'Got you. Got you at last … I am Death. No one escapes my clutch.' A version of this story can be found in Betty Rosen's *And None of it was Nonsense. The Power of Storytelling in School* (Rosen 1988:94-6). This book is a classic and should be read by all who feel the need for a powerful rationale before embarking on storytelling for the first time. It is an inspirational account of her work and a helpful resource.

I associate all my best stories with the person I first heard telling it. Storytelling events, conferences and even watching TV can be excellent resources and introduce you to new stories. A Theatre in Education (TIE) group visiting a school where I was teaching in 1990 did a wonderful performance of *The Firebird* and started an interest in the Russian stories of Baba Yaga. For weeks, the children were fascinated by the idea of Baba Yaga the witch with iron teeth and a house on a chicken's leg and they told and retold the story they had heard, particularly when they were playing outside at break time. I can never tell the story of Daedalus and Icarus without remembering eight year old Yasmin's version and the way her body enacted the words, 'down, down, down he came into the ocean ...' arms gracefully held above her head as she gently subsided on the floor. Another memorable occasion for me occurred when a De Montfort student contributed to a storytelling session. She enchanted a large group of students by telling them a Guyanese story that she had heard from her grandmother. It was one of the many stories about the trickster Anansi and told how the owl came to have such big eyes and such a mournful cry. This was in punishment for a trick that Anansi had encouraged him to play on the women of the village. The student told the story in creole and explained the ritual call of 'cric-crac' to alert the audience that a tale was about to begin. She set the scene for the telling by dividing the audience into two halves and taught each half a brief musical phrase which they sang in harmony as an introduction to the story. In this way she drew them into the tale as a community of listeners.

Anecdotes and stories of personal experience

All the stories I have mentioned above are part of an oral tradition being endlessly told and retold. At the same time there are other stories which are more personal and local: the stories of our communities and families. Some of these become apocryphal and part of an ongoing local oral tradition. Where I live a lot of neighbourhood shops are closing down, with boarded up or painted over windows. Speculation about what may be going to happen to them is rife and a number of rival views are exchanged when people meet on the street; these often involve an elaborate mini story, some extended by reminiscences about what the neighbourhood used to be like before the coming of out-of-town supermarkets. Exchanging these stories enables neighbours to feel part of a community; a community of speculation, reminiscence and narrative.

We may become part of our local community by sharing stories but we discover who we are through the narratives of our family. Some stories take on the status of the written word. They have been told so often that they cannot be altered. My mother's story of how she travelled across Europe and the Mediterranean to a country called Persia in the 1920s, can be confidently retold by her daughters to their children. Like the photograph album, the tales we hear about ourselves and our families shape our identity. Every family is a network of stories criss-crossing the generations.

Storytelling in the National Curriculum and the National Literacy Strategy

There has never been a better time for storytelling. In the revised National Curriculum, the requirements for Speaking and Listening have been clarified; there are specific requirements relating to drama and more significantly there is an alignment between the programmes of study for Key Stages 1 and 2 and the *National Literacy Strategy Framework for Teaching*. This means that storytelling is more securely embedded in the curriculum and has regained some of the status it seemed to have lost after 1988.

Looking at the programme of study for Key Stage 1, the *Range* of speaking includes 'telling stories real and imagined' and drama activities include, 'presenting ... stories to others'. Under *Skills* both the requirements to 'speak clearly and confidently' and to 'listen, understand and respond to others', will be met by hearing and telling stories where the need to speak with 'clear diction, to choose words with precision, organise what they say and take into account the needs of their listeners is self-evident. As far as drama activities are concerned, storytelling will provide the vehicle for 'using language and actions to convey situations, characters and emotions' (DfEE 1999:14-15).

At Key Stage 2, the emphasis is on enabling pupils 'to sustain their contributions in different contexts, adapting their talk to a range of purposes and audiences'. Taking on different roles as they tell stories will help to develop the confidence to present to different audiences; it will also help them 'to use characters, action and narrative to convey story, themes, and emotions' in what will become more structured scripted plays. At the same time, all this will contribute to their understanding and experience of how language varies according to context and purpose (DfEE 1999:19-20).

At both Key Stages the extent to which storytelling contributes to pupils' written English should not be underestimated: at Key Stage 1 pupils are required to be able 'to communicate meaning in narrative' and 'sequence events and recount them in appropriate detail' (DfEE 1999: 17-18) and, at Key Stage 2, to use a language and style appropriate to the reader and to develop ideas into structured written texts (DfEE 1999: 23), both of which can draw on experiences of oral storytelling.

The National Literacy Strategy Framework for Teaching (DfEE 1998) is closely related to the English Order and provides a more detailed basis for implementing the statutory requirements of the programmes of study. The focus is on Reading and Writing but in the Reception Year we find that considerable emphasis is placed on the development of oral storytelling: 'Pupils should be taught to use knowledge of familiar texts to re-enact or re-tell to others, recounting the main points in correct sequence' and 'to be aware of story structures e.g. actions/reactions, consequences and the ways that stories are built up and concluded'. In Year 1 Term 1 this is continued; they are 'to re-enact stories in a variety of ways e.g. through role play, using dolls or puppets'. In Term 2, they 'should be taught to re-tell stories, giving the main points in sequence' and should practise using some of the key features of story language in oral retellings. In Term 3, they are 'to prepare and re-tell stories orally, identifying and using some of the more formal features of story language.' Early literacy development is seen to be dependent on a rich diet of stories read aloud and told. The National Literacy Strategy (NLS) implicitly acknowledges the significance of spoken language in this process. In Year 2 Term 2, although the emphasis has shifted from telling to writing, we still find that 'pupils should be taught to prepare and re-tell stories individually and through role play in groups using dialogue ...'. In Year 3 Term 1, pupils should 'be aware of the different voices using dramatised readings showing differences between narrator and different characters used e.g. puppets to present stories'. This would clearly benefit from an oral as well as written approach. In Year 3 Term 3, under Reading and Comprehension strategies, pupils should be taught to 're-tell main points of story in sequence; to compare different stories ...'. In the first three years of schooling the National Literacy Strategy systematically lays the foundation for increasingly sophisticted skills of comprehension and composition at text level in which oral storytelling can play a significant role. By Year 5 Term 2 children are required to become familiar with traditional stories, myths, legends and fables from a range of cultures. They will be expected to be able to 'identify and classify the features of myths, legends and fables' and to 'explore the similarities and differences between oral and written storytelling'. Developing skill as tellers of stories will inform both the comprehension and composition of literary texts; practical experience will inform the analysis and construction of texts. Although the activities listed above only represent a very thin strand of text level work in the framework for teaching, it is nevertheless a significant one, which usefully overlaps with the requirements for drama in the National Curriculum.

Storytelling and literacy

While the National Literacy Strategy framework may seem to make little explicit reference to oracy, it is acknowledged that Speaking and Listening do provide the foundation for literacy, and the National Curriculum makes this explicit. What the Literacy Strategy does make clear, however, is the contribution that oral storytelling makes both to the development of writing and of reading; through telling stories children learn about their structure, the significance of the setting, the role of characterisation, and the power of the language; they learn to use language to create an effect on an audience. For all children there will be, at least initially, 'a gap ... between what they can say and what they can comfortably produce in writing' (Fox 1993:65). Looking at children's oral and written versions of the same story, we can see how much more confidently they use storytelling techniques in an oral rather than a written version. But it is also interesting to see how dependent an oral version can be on previously heard written versions. Eight year old Rhian writes a story, 'The Party in Transylvania', (Slater 1995):

> Long long ago lived a Dracula in his castle he lived with his mother and his freind called frankensein Dracula woke up at 8 o'clock and he woke his freind up at 10 o. clock Nora Rock cooked lunch at 12.o.clock he had his lunch 3.p.m and he was bored so he decided to take his dogs for a walk through the forest there was a fall moon to night cries Mr Wolf that night in the same castle they held a big party one of the gusts ask Nora Rock for a dance grow up good night says Dracula Thend

Rhian wrote this story a week after she had told a story called 'Dracula in Pennsylvania [sic]' to a small group of friends. The oral version is quite different, much longer and uses a wider range of linguistic features. It starts, 'one stormy night in the land of Transylvania Dracula was having his lunch and he said to his servant go and find a chunky pig for me to eat and a ghost done it and he found it wasn't really a chunky pig it was this fat, sweetish meat ball'. The story continues, providing a girl character, 'this woman fell down this really big hole and she turned into a girl half way through the hole'. The girl then has to contend with ghosts, much screaming and a range of horrors, 'the floor started creaking and she looked up and there were spider webs everywhere', and later her mother meets a horrible end, 'they didn't know who tore her to pieces'. All of this lurid fantasy is most probably drawn from Rhian's experience of TV cartoons but it also has a fluency and dramatic pace that is lacking in her written version. Also, telling the story was a social event with immediate response from a peer group who share her evident delight in ghostly horrors and violence, blood and death. The written version, mainly for the teacher's eyes, is a very sedate, domesticated version of Dracula living at home with his mum and feeling, as Rhian probably does under similar circumstances, rather bored. Although we can see the influence of traditional tales, 'Long ago lived a Dracula in his castle', and 'there was a full moon', the story has little structure whereas the oral tale has considerable momentum and confidently uses a number of literary devices to carry the story forward:

> 'when the girl screamed, it frightened the ghost so much that the ghost fainted and turned into two twin ghosts and the girl ran home and told her mother that there was a ghost in the castle and her mother said, 'Now I don't believe in ghosts, I'm sure there's a mis ...' She heard this noise go OOOH, OOOH and the floor started creaking and she looked up and there was spider webs everywhere and the spiders turned into these gigantic spiders and they ate this woman up and they tore her to pieces and then there was all blood and guts floating in the house, and this girl, her little daughter came back and her dad said 'Where's Mum?' And the little girl said, 'I don't know where Mum is'.

This is a pretty powerful story that owes a great deal, in language and structure, to fairy tales and folk stories that she may have heard, as well as the scary cartoon versions of these stories that she enjoys on TV. Unlike the very unsatisfactory ending of the written story, where the party promised in the title only appears as an afterthought, the oral version provides a satisfactory resolution and closure, 'and that's how nobody believes in ghosts'. It is a far more accomplished story which tells us a lot about her understanding of narrative technique. As her teacher suggests, if we only take her written version into account, 'Rhian's linguistic capabilities may well be underestimated' (Slater 1995). But maybe we also need to ask why Rhian is telling this story at all. It starts conventionally with Dracula in his castle but the focus quickly shifts to a little girl in confrontation with gigantic spiders and ghosts. She encounters supernatural dangers and death. Told with relish and bravado to an enthusiastic audience, it is nonetheless a story about loss, 'And the little girl said, "I don't know where Mum is"'. It deals with every child's greatest nightmare – the death of a parent. In telling this story she could be coming to terms with a real fear which her audience will recognise and share (Bettelheim 1991). Telling a story of this kind allows her to reflect on frightening issues in safety, even to mock them. As Betty Rosen suggests, 'The symbolic representation of fearsome things through the safe medium of folk story may well help the intent listener to come to terms with real life pain' (Rosen 1991:31). In the same way, stories that children tell may contribute to their emotional development. If this is the case, it is another powerful argument for using storytelling in the classroom, not only as an instrument for supporting development in reading and writing, but as a means to help children to shape and control their understanding of the world.

From oral to written versions and back again

In the story told by Rhian, it is impossible to tell exactly where it came from as it is not a direct retelling of a particular story but draws on a range of experiences, of stories heard and read, and of everyday speech. When Mum says, 'Now I don't believe in ghosts. I'm sure there's a mistake' we can hear the sceptical adult voice that she is mimicking. When children write they draw as much on what they hear in the everyday world, the idiom, the cadences of speech, as they do on the written mode which they hear in the stories that are read to them. David, aged seven, writes, 'Yesterday my sister broc her arm we were playing a game like this'. He then adds a small drawing to illustrate the accident. One of the characters is lying down with 'ou ou ou' written beside her, another is saying, 'its all right darling', in a speech balloon. The story continues:

> So we went to nanny we had to get to the hospital qiclee. when we got there she was all right till they did there thing to her she was scremin you could hear it from the other side of the hospital Then she was crying and stoping then she was carm.Then we went home, And now she has some stuf on her and a sling and she's all right now.

This story seems heavily dependent on an oral mode, what Michael Rosen has described as 'the continuity between the oral tradition and personal writing' (Rosen 1989: 25). David writes as if he is speaking to us, offering his drawing as a short cut to describe what he must have experienced as a moment of panic and confusion, soothed by what he must have heard over the noise of his sister's crying, nanny's calming 'It's all right, darling'. As he continues the tale he seems to pick up the rhythm of adult voices telling the story over a cup of tea, 'we had to get there quickly', 'you could hear it from the other side of the hospital', 'she's all right now'. It is a story he has heard as it has been retold and shaped in the oral culture of his family. Now it has become part of his own repertoire and has contributed to his oral and written expertise.

David: Aged 7 years 1 month.

Tuesday 5th may

yesterday My sister Broke her arm
we were Playing a game
like this.

ts all right darling

so we you ou to mamy
we had went to get
to the hospitel a icee.
when we got there
she was all right
till they did there thing
to her she was seremin
you could hear it from
the oter side of the hospitel
The she was crying and
stoping then she was calm.
then we went
home. And now
she has some stuf
on her and a sling
and she's all right
now.

The playground: a site for storytelling

Many stories have their origins in the home and are part of a shared family culture; others have had their origins in the peer culture outside the classroom and are most easily observed on the school playground. Talking to two eleven year olds, they remembered the games they played on their lower school playground:

> Jess: we always used to do plays, didn't we? We had a little secret place we'd go in, somewhere round the corner …
> Lucy: Oh yeah and we used to make up plays
> Jess: and everybody got kidnapped and things … I can remember we used to play fairies …
> Lucy: I remember, do you remember when we used to play schools with Lyn …
> Jess: and we always used to play mums and dads
> Lucy: and you were always the mum …
> (Grugeon 1988)

While the girls sometimes play rather domestic games, groups of boys often play a chasing game which they call *Cops and Robbers*. Games like this often involve complex narratives and seem to exist on every playground. A researcher engaged in auditing the way space is used by children on playgrounds has found evidence of a thriving narrative tradition. He has shown that primary school playgrounds reflect the texts of stories being played. On most playgrounds children will identify particular features relating to these narrative games, such as the jail or prison in *Cops and Robbers*: this may be a particular bit of the school fence, or some descending steps may become a dungeon. Then there will be a witch's house, used particularly by younger children during pretend games of good versus evil. Small features in the playground, such as drain covers, would be identified as the cooking pots and furnaces for cooking bad boys and girls. Children would always tell this researcher about the ghosts and spooky characters who inhabit the primary school toilet block (Armitage 1998).

Children's oral culture

The extended narratives that accompany role-play games, are often based on the players' recent TV or film experience; at the time of writing *Star Wars* and *Bugs* are popular and computer games and TV cartoons continue to offer inspiration. This has evidently always been the case as the Opies' extensive scholarly studies of playground lore and language have shown (1959, 1984, 1985). My daughter at the age of five, 20 years ago, came home from school with her first playground rhyme:

Batman and Robin
In the batmobile
Batman did a fart
And paralysed the wheel.
The wheel wouldn't go
The engine wouldn't start
All because of Batman
And his supersonic fart.

She was delighted by the naughtiness of this little rhyme; and we might notice that it has a narrative structure that is far more complex, and vocabulary that is more challenging, than the typical text of a school reading scheme. She and her friends were to go on to develop a considerable repertoire of narratives during their early years on the playground. These would introduce them to a number of narrative and syntactic conventions: 'Down in the town where nobody goes /Lives an old lady who washes her clothes …' 'One day as I was walking, I heard my boyfriend talking', 'If your teacher interferes/Turn her up and box her ears …' all of which could be used in more formal storytelling contexts. Five year olds today are not interested in Batman; he has been superseded by other media texts:

Postman Pat, Postman Pat
Postman Pat ran over his cat.
Blood and guts were flying
Postman Pat was crying
And all blood ran over
Poor Pat's van. (1995)

This subversive parody of the Postman Pat song has intertextual links with Rhian's Dracula story where, 'there was guts and blood floating in the house' and reflects the fascination and fear that seem to impel young children to tell stories and play games that confront some of their deepest anxieties. The persistent media influence is continued in the frequent appearance across the UK since 1997 of a number of songs sung to the tune of 'Nick nack paddy whack,' mocking the Teletubbies:

I love you.You love me
Together we'll kill Dipsy
With a dagger through his heart
And a bullet through his head
Sorry La La, Dipsy's dead. (1997)

What these rhymes share with traditional tales is a love of the ribald, a celebration of the upturning of everyday life and an enjoyment in naughty, daring, rude and frightening events. They provide a secure framework for the exploration of mutual feelings, hopes and fears. Rhymes, games, jokes, gossip, everyday events, all provide a context for young children to become experts in the narrative mode, and a rich resource for more formal opportunities provided by the school. At the heart of the fast moving acquisition of cognitive and affective skills and understanding during the early years is story. Story, whether in the playground, in the classroom or on television is all one in being a vital element in children's personal growth and development and in the confident acquisition of skills required for literate competence.

References

Armitage, Marc (1998) 'The Ins and Outs of Playground Play: the Relationship of the Physical Environment to Imaginative Play'. Unpublished paper, *The State of Play*. Conference: Sheffield University.

Bettelheim, Bruno (1991) *The Uses of Enchantment: the Meaning and Importance of Fairy Tales*. London: Pergamon.

Aylwin, A. (1992) Traditional Storytelling and Education. London: University of Greenwich.

Britton, James (1970) *Language and Learning*. London: Allen Lane.

Colwell, Eileen (1990) *Storytelling*. Stroud: The Thimble Press.

DfEE (1998) *The National Literacy Strategy Framework for Teaching*. London: DfEE.

DfEE (1999) *The Proposals for the Revised National Curriculum*. London: QCA Publications.

Fox, Carol (1993) *At the Very Edge of the Forest: the Influence of Literature on Storytelling by Children*. London: Cassell.

Garvie, Edie (1990) *Story as Vehicle: Teaching English to Young Children*. Clevedon: Multilingual Matters.

Graham, Judith (1990) *Pictures on the Page*. Sheffield: NATE

Grainger, Teresa (1997) *Traditional Storytelling in the Primary Classroom*. Leamington Spa: Scholastic.

Gregory, Eve (1996) *Making Sense of a New World: Learning to Read in a Second Language*. London: Paul Chapman Publishing.

Grugeon, E. (1988) 'Children's oral culture: a transitional experience', in McClure, M. *et al. Oracy Matters*. Milton Keynes: Open University Press.

Grugeon, E. *et al.* (1998) *Teaching Speaking and Listening in the Primary School*. London: David Fulton Publishers.

Medlicott, Mary (ed.) (1989) *By Word of Mouth: the Revival of Storytelling*. C4 Broadside Publications.

Meek, Margaret (1990) *On Being Literate*. London: Bodley Head.

Opie, I. and Opie, P. (1959) *The Lore and Language of Schoolchildren*. Oxford: Oxford University Press.

Opie, I. and Opie, P. (1984) *Children's Games in Street and Playground*. Oxford: Oxford University Press.

Opie, I. and Opie, P.(1985) *The Singing Game*. Oxford: Oxford University Press.

Rosen, Betty (1988) *And None of it was Nonsense: the Power of Storytelling in School*. London: Mary Glasgow Publications.

Rosen, Betty (1991) *Shapers and Polishers: Teachers as Storytellers*. London: Mary Glasgow Publications.

Rosen, Harold (1985) *Stories and Meanings*. Sheffield: NATE Publications.

Rosen, Michael (1989) *Did I hear you write?* London: André Deutsch.

Slater (neé Taylor), Vikki (1995) 'Can Children's Playground Culture Contribute to their Classroom Experience?' Unpublished BEd Dissertation, De Montfort University.

CHAPTER 2

Reading about storytelling

Learning from the experts

Most of us do not have the time or opportunity to listen to professional storytellers in action but we can still become confident and competent storytellers by following the example of a number of practitioners who have written about their own experiences or have seriously researched issues related to narrative and storytelling. There are a number of excellent books which look at storytelling from different perspectives and which can contribute to our understanding about the importance of story in the development of literacy skills and add to our repertoire. The books I shall refer to now are all texts which have influenced my understanding over a period of years.

Certainly not nonsense

Top of my list is Betty Rosen's *And None of it was Nonsense: The Power of Storytelling in School*. Although this is an account of work in an inner city secondary boys' school, the message for primary school teachers is clear: powerful stories with universal messages about human concerns, such as jealousy, love, power, magic, fairness, will evoke powerful responses from young people. When these often archetypal stories are told very directly and then retold and reshaped by the listeners the effects can be dramatic – as Rosen illustrates in her account of the boys' response to the different stories she told them. She writes:

> To use storytelling as a major way of teaching and learning there must be above all else, the certainty that children (all children, all people) have the capacity to transform and create out of what they receive. Most English teachers assume this up to a point when they try to inspire children to write after reading poetry, stories, plays and novels with them … But to close the books, look at the kids, tell them

a story from scratch, then ask them to tell that story back again puts the whole process into a new dimension. It presupposes an enormous confidence in people to know that something new and good will come from every child.

(Rosen, B. 988:8)

Her book describes how this process of transformation and creation happened in her classroom – but only with a great deal of careful preparation. I have always found the following helpful:

There is no doubt that there is such a category as the 'born' storyteller but if like me, you are not a natural in the field, then let me share my lesson preparation with you.

Here is the basic foursome:

- Find a story you like massively; a story your imagination will relish, cherish and nourish.
- Get all the facts and details together, even those you will later reject: there's a lot of lesson preparation involved, although with luck, your pupils will never guess.
- Decide what you are going to include, note it down in sequence and, in the process, consider particularly carefully how you are going to begin.
- Visualise the start precisely; by this I mean allow the opening situation to occupy – take over – your imagination. This will go a long way towards ensuring that you will speak with your own voice a story that has become your own …

Essentially the story must become your own before you retell it, 'revisioned' by you so that your reception of it becomes a complete creative act.

(Rosen, B. 1988:54-5)

Rosen illustrates this process of recreation as she describes how she shared powerful stories with a challenging group of boys from a range of cultures and backgrounds. In a postscript to Betty Rosen's book, Harold Rosen puts her experience into a broader perspective.

For this book is more than a description of classroom practices centred around narratives. It is a demonstration of the uncanny power of narrative as a means of presenting, analysing and weighing experiences, the teacher's experiences of using narrative as a focus of classroom practice. It is an autobiographical story of stories. It is one long meta-narrative – the name which has been given to all those features of a story which refer to the story itself.

(Rosen, B. 1988:163-4)

Making sense of the world

It was from Harold Rosen, at a National Oracy Project conference in 1989, that I had learned how storytelling is a means by which very young children make sense of their lives. In order to do this they have to identify and select significant details among the mass of impressions and experiences that seem to bombard them in a relatively undifferentiated way and then shape and order them. I came to understand that storytelling is a profoundly important part of a child's cognitive development. Narrative, Harold Rosen suggests, 'is nothing if not a supreme means of rendering otherwise chaotic, shapeless events into a coherent whole, saturated with meaning' (1988:164). He proceeds to demonstrate that behind this statement is 'a whole universe of scholarly thought' (1988:165) and supports this assertion by reference to the work of Hardy, Jamison, Baumann and Bruner. In summary he suggests that

> ... stories do not offer single meanings. They form interlocking sets of meanings and listening to a story is a search for these meanings through the meanings we already possess. In retelling, we both repeat the words of others and change them. Even our own personal stories we change in new contexts, carrying forward some of the old, but shifting, however slightly, the meanings of the story. We are incorrigible reworkers of our own and other people's stories.
> (Rosen, H. in Rosen, B. 1988:170)

Betty Rosen is an incorrigible reworker of stories and having looked at children telling stories, continued her work to produce a sequel, *Shapers and Polishers: Teachers as Storytellers* (1991) which not only convinces us that there are very good reasons for having a go ourselves, but also contains 12 powerful stories to tell in the classroom. It is particularly interesting in what it has to say about telling tales that explore personal experience and autobiographical storytelling. As she notes:

> Our identity is made up from an amalgam of those past experiences, right up to the present and into the imagined future. To make sense of ourselves for ourselves, not only do we select from our memories but we invent beginnings and endings for them which do not exist as such in the continuous flow of our living. Thus the storyteller inside each head constructs the tale.
> (Rosen, B. 1991:56)

'Our own and other people's stories' do indeed seem to make up the world we live in to a far greater extent than we tend to realise. This morning, I have probably discussed last night's episodes of *Coronation*

Street and *EastEnders* with family or friends. Both of these soaps are stories of high drama that have their origins in far more ancient stories of jealousy and intrigue. On TV recently, a discussion in the interval of a performance of Handel's opera *Semele*, the story of Jupiter, king of the gods' seduction of a mortal woman, pointedly related the story to the epic tale of Monica and President Clinton – the parallels were all too obvious. Literary criticism has shown us that there are no new stories, only reworkings of archetypal myths; the stories we hear and tell are all part of an intertextual web.

Learning the language of storytelling

Carol Fox's scholarly study of the storytelling skills of very young children, *At the Very Edge of the Forest*, draws on the work of a number of literary theorists. Her very detailed multi-layered analysis of stories told by five children reveals layers of complexity in the children's story structures. She explores the language of their stories at the level of the word, the sentence, the plot structure, the structure of the discourse and the way these stories reflect the children's thinking. This study provides the most detailed and compelling evidence to illustrate the importance of narrative in young children's development; it underlines the importance of the stories that they hear and have read to them to their future thinking, reading and writing.

Universal truths

This seems to be particularly significant for pupils who are in the process of acquiring English as an additional language. We know that pupils take on and reproduce the larger units of discourse, such as story forms, before they give attention to details of lexical, syntactic and phonological correctness. 'Pupils in the process of learning English seem to benefit most from internalising the typical rhythms and cadences of different kinds of discourse ... stories told and read to them.' (Levine, J. in Meek, M. 1996:69). Eve Gregory, in *Making Sense of a New World: Learning to Read in a Second Language*, emphasises the value of traditional folk and fairy tales and fables, 'for affective, cognitive and linguistic reasons. They introduce children and their families into a new cultural heritage, yet contain familiar morals and values the world over' (Gregory 1996:134). In this immensely rewarding and thought-provoking book the contribution of the told story for both monolingual and emergent bilinguals to the process of learning to read is convincingly presented. She asserts that 'teachers know that most memorable stories contain universal truths, values and morals …' and she suggests questions that teachers might consider as they choose stories:

- Will the story interest the children? Is it memorable?
- Will the story motivate the children by drawing on their personal experience or emotions? Will it develop their imagination and/or appeal to their sense of humour?
- Is there a strong and exciting or appealing storyline which will hold the children's interest in spite of not understanding all the language used?
- Will the story arouse their curiosity and help them respond positively to the target culture, language and language learning? If there are any specific cultural references, are they clear?
- Is the language level appropriate? Is it clear and unambiguous? Does it make sense without relying on children's ability to understand complex structures and/or colloquialisms? Is it memorable i.e. does it contain features such as rhyme, onomatopoeia, rhythm and encourage appropriate use of intonation patterns which will help the children's pronunciation?
- Is there natural repetition to help the children to participate in the text, facilitate memorising and provide pronunciation practice? Does the repetition enable the children to predict what is coming next in the story?

(Gregory 1996:122)

These seem to be key questions that we should be asking whenever we make decisions about the stories we choose to tell. This list was intended to offer some criteria for book selection for teachers in multilingual classrooms but it seems equally appropriate for the selection of stories to be told orally in any classroom as it reminds us of the way stories are mediators of language and culture.

Memorable stories

In my personal quest to become both a storyteller and a teacher of storytellers to be, another book that I have found inspirational is Edie Garvie's *Story as Vehicle: Teaching English to Young Children* (1990). I once attended an in-service training course where she explained and demonstrated her belief in story as a vehicle on the journey of teaching and learning English as an additional language. She told a story, a tale from the Indian sub-continent, and demonstrated its potential, even in those days long before the arrival of the National Literacy Strategy, for detailed work at word, sentence and text level. She introduced the practical idea of providing 'story packs' by loading the vehicle with a collection of teaching aids based on a particular story; a pack would typically contain such items as a version of the story, a cassette recording, pictures and charts, word and sentence cards, worksheets and suggestions for lessons. Story packs could be available to all staff in a school and be prepared by teachers or classroom assistants. The important thing about these packs is that they would be specifically designed to meet the particular linguistic needs of a group of children and that they would arise from stories which also met those children's needs in terms of their cultural background and the relevant issues and themes they might raise. The choice of appropriate story must always come first as the vehicle; related activities Garvie refers to as the 'trailer'. Her book is full of practical ideas for stories and resources but her detailed story methodology is grounded in a theory of learning and teaching which she has developed over many years in the context of English as a Second Language/English as a Foreign Language (ESL/EFL) teaching in the UK and overseas. Her advice to the teacher storyteller is to:

1. Build up a resource bank of potential stories across a number of genres and a number of cultures.
2. Bearing in mind the learning journey, all the issues, build up a repertoire of ideas and a collection of prototype materials as props for the narration and equipment for the follow up.
3. For any particular purpose, select an appropriate story and turn it into narrative for the classroom, loading it with the special issues required. If necessary do the narrative at more than one level.
4. At the same time select judiciously from the follow up resources for the immediate aftermath and the rest of the trailer.
5. Return to the story, presenting work to challenge and extend the original learning.
6. If this particular story works well, consider keeping the materials selected together in a fairly permanent kit, making notes to remind yourself and others of why this or that was opted for.
7. Keep revising your resource banks, bringing them up to date.

(Garvie 1990:128)

Narrative and pictures

Sometimes, we can find important references to narrative and storytelling in books that focus on a different topic. In *What's in the Picture? Responding to Illustrations in Picture Books* (Evans 1998) two chapters reinforce the importance of storytelling and emphasise the way looking at pictures supports the development of narrative competence. In 'A way into a new language and culture', Liz Laycock explores the contribution that picture books can make to the successful acquisition of a new language; she illustrates the way that the interactive sharing of picture books enables children to draw on existing skills of storytelling in both their community language and their new language as they attempt to retell the story that they can see in the pictures. She stresses the need for versions of traditional fairy stories to be part of classroom provision alongside traditional stories from other cultures: 'There is so much literature in English which presupposes a knowledge of traditional tales that they are a necessary part of the acculturation process.' (Evans, 1998:85).

In her chapter, 'Turning the visual into the verbal: children reading wordless books', Judith Graham demonstrates how 'in the reading or "beholding" of a wordless picture book, the reader becomes the narrator, with all that implies for cocreating and bonding to the book' (Evans 1998:30) but she also suggests that this is much less straightforward than we have been inclined to believe. She found that children attempting to retell the story that they 'saw' in a wordless text found structuring a coherent tale surprisingly difficult; they tended to record the events as a running commentary. However, when they were encouraged to draw on their existing skills as storytellers and form a narrative using the past tense, starting with 'once upon a time' and taking on 'the traditional all-seeing, all-knowing narrator's role', the move from the visual to the verbal was much more assured, they were able to tell the story of the pictures. If we give readers of wordless books, Graham argues, 'the optimum conditions in which to study the books and in which to fashion a verbal telling, wordless books can confirm children as competent interpreters and as fluent and creative language users' (Evans 1998:42-3). Both Laycock and Graham present illuminating studies of children's storytelling experiences in the classroom.

Traditional tales

Teresa Grainger's *Traditional Storytelling in the Primary Classroom* is a practical guide for teachers which is deeply informed by recent theory. She seeks to encourage and inspire teachers to 'reinstate traditional oral storytelling as a powerful form of education and provide children with the chance to develop their natural capacity and become the official storytellers in the classroom' (Grainger 1997:9) and she sets out to illustrate the potential of traditional tales to contribute to language learning; the emphasis is on establishing a storytelling ethos in the classroom. 'Personal and traditional tales represent the resource bank for retelling which the teacher can help the class establish, share and widen'

(1997:59). There is much that will be of immediate practical use in the classroom; anthologies, picture books and audio-cassettes are recommended; ideas for developing reading and writing activities are suggested; units of work on traditional storytelling in the context of national curricula are indicated; the important link with role play and drama is illustrated. At the heart of the text are eight powerful tales from around the world for retelling. It is a book which bubbles with very informed commitment and enthusiasm:

> Learning to tell stories in the classroom is very worthwhile and extremely satisfying. After the tale has been selected, its shape committed to memory and practised, it is ready to be played into existence in interaction with the audience. The voice is used in an instrumental and creative manner alongside gesture, pace, music and/or artefacts to share the flavour and spirit of the tale. This combination of commitment to the tale, a playful attitude and personal conviction in the truth of the story lies at the heart of storytelling.
> (Grainger 1997:60)

Developing language skills

Another impressively informed practical text which teachers will find particularly helpful is Claire Jennings' *Children as Storytellers: Developing Language Skills in the Classroom* (1991). The book is based on Jennings' experience of storytelling workshops in Australian classrooms where we see children grow in confidence as language users in response to the activities that she describes: 'A successful story always has its origins in oracy … if children are to become confident with their literacy skills then we must allow them to share their ideas first' (1991:1). It is an approach which we are to see again and again in this book that will have value for children with English as a second language. She is particularly concerned with raising the profile of storytelling as 'a vehicle for developing not only spoken language but also the self-esteem and social skills of all children' (1991:9). Her chapter 'Strategies to develop awareness of story features' (1991:30-41) will be particularly useful to teachers of Year 5 and Year 6 in the UK, who are currently required by both the National Curriculum and the National Literacy Strategy Framework for Teaching to provide children with a detailed understanding of narrative structure. Of particular relevance is the suggestion, 'If we can help them to realise the puzzles and powers of the characters, not just as they appear on the surface, but also their essence, their inner thoughts and how their actions determine the outcome of the story, then we are equipping children to conquer the world of narrative' (1991:31). There are also strategies to enhance children's understanding of setting, plot, character and visual imagery. The activities suggested are all to be used in the context of storytelling itself and intended to 'equip children with tools for experimenting with the elements of story and to give them greater power over oral and written samples of their own' (1991:41).

The National Oracy Project

In the late 1980s and early 1990s the National Oracy Project (NOP) was a catalyst for a considerable revival of storytelling in primary schools. Teachers in primary and secondary schools in a number of local education authorities began to work with storytelling and professional storytellers more confidently; ideas were shared nationally through regular NOP publications, a newsletter, *Oracy Issues,* and a journal, *Talk.* Local newsletters disseminated successful practice and ideas.These ranged from providing every child with audio cassettes, as you might with exercise books for writing, equipping classrooms with an adequate supply of cassette recorders, providing small sound proofed areas for recording (these were sometimes ingenious constructions), organising storytelling events between classes and schools, awarding certificates for success in storytelling and generally giving storytelling a high profile. In response to this, there was evidence of a new interest in storytelling and in traditional tales. 'From the educators' point of view, it highlighted the applications of storytelling on an unprecedented scale. From the storytellers' point of view, the Project afforded unrivalled opportunities to acquire professional experience and knowledge ...' (Heywood 1998:32) Much of this was later abandoned in favour of more narrowly conceived ideas in response to the National Curriculum. However, there has been a lasting legacy of good practice in many schools and the habit of funding professional storytellers in school persists (1998:33). Among the publications emerging from the NOP, one is a tribute to the energy and investment of teachers and pupils who contributed to the development of storytelling in education during the project. *Common Bonds: Storytelling in the Classroom* (Howe and Johnson 1992) locates storytelling in the context of National Curriculum requirements and draws together the work of hundreds of teachers from England and Wales who had been developing approaches to storytelling in all areas of the curriculum; it provides an unprecedented resource and an affirmation of the power of storytelling in the classroom. Defining storytelling as a broad and inclusive range of activities in which all pupils can participate, it offers practical guidance and advice and looks reflectively at case-study materials which provide evidence of ways in which the narrative mode can be built into the learning of pupils across the curriculum.

> We have put the case for storytelling as a powerful way of developing language and learning ... we have seen how valuable a resource stories can be for helping pupils shape their experiences, and for deepening their understanding of the world. We have shown how both pupils and teachers can grow in confidence as tellers of stories themselves.
>
> (Howe and Johnson 1992: 68)

Pioneers

All the books referred to above owe a debt to earlier writers such as Eileen Colwell and Bob Barton. In *Storytelling*, Colwell draws on the experience of telling tales in libraries and elsewhere since the 1920s. Eileen Colwell is a pioneer storyteller who is reassuringly convinced that we can all follow her example.

> Some rare individuals are natural storytellers and are able to tell stories with ease and confidence. Most people, however, are unsure of their ability while others are even convinced that storytelling is totally beyond them. This is a fallacy, for anyone who is willing to spend some time in study and practise can become a good storyteller. As in life, you can only learn by trial and error, and encouragement is vital if you are to gain confidence.
>
> (Colwell 1991:17) (also 1980)

And she offers the most detailed and wise advice and encouragement, drawing on years of experience. In the new edition of her book (1991) she documents a revival of storytelling in the 1980s as a world wide phenomenon and rejoices in

> the revival and dissemination of stories to all age groups ... where in the main traditional material is used which helps keep alive the ethnic folk literature so important for the shifting populations of the world today.The exchange of stories helps communication not only between cultures but between generations. Storytelling is a force in the modern world as it was in the ancient world.
>
> (Colwell 1991:91) (also 1980)

Bob Barton, in *Tell Me Another: Storytelling and Reading Aloud at Home, at School and in the Community* (1986), draws on twenty-five years of telling stories as a teacher and, like Colwell, believes that 'the potential to tell a story is in everyone' and that 'a willingness to explore and experiment is one of the greatest assets you can bring to the task of storytelling' (1986:8). And like Colwell, he also believes that while we 'are all natural storytellers' many of us 'lack confidence to get up in front of a group and tell one' and he sets out to offer practical encouragement. Through personal stories of his classroom experience, he presents us with a very rich resource and rationale for choosing different approaches to traditional tales and contemporary stories, suggesting a variety of active ways in which we can involve the children in participating in the story: chanting, singing, acting.

Making meaning: narrative and young children

Two other writers who have contributed to the theory which underpins our understanding of the role of narrative in language development and reading progress are Gordon Wells and Jerome Bruner. In *The Meaning Makers: Children Learning Language and Using Language to Learn* (1987) Wells provides evidence of the powerful influence of an early experience of hearing stories in the home on language acquisition and fluency. In *Actual Minds, Possible Worlds* (1986) Bruner develops ideas which have become immensely influential in the primary school: the theory of 'scaffolding' and that of 'joint culture creation', both of which can be seen to support the role of story in the primary curriculum.

Conclusion

No amount of advice about the best way to tell tales, nor an elaborate rationale for doing it, is of any use, however without the raw material, the stories themselves. The books referred to so far have extensive lists and references and often contain a number of stories and traditional tales for telling. However, it would be a pity to end the chapter without reference to some of the talented tellers themselves who have, through their own performance, done much to raise the profile of storytelling in schools and have produced their own anthologies. Grace Hallworth's wonderful collection of Caribbean tales in *Mouth Open, Story Jump Out*, Beulah Candappa's *Tales of South Asia* and Mary Medlicott's collection of tales from around the world, *Time for Telling,* make a good starting point for the novice storyteller.

Indeed, this chapter has been written for a novice storyteller who might want to understand why and how storytelling can make such powerful contribution to education. It offers an overview of the way the art of storytelling in the classroom has evolved in recent years. All the writers above have made a significant contribution to our understanding of the value of oral storytelling and many provide practical advice for the primary classroom. The next chapter looks at the way some teachers developed their skills as they explored the potential for storytelling in their classrooms.

References

Barton, Bob (1986) *Tell Me Another: Storytelling and Reading Aloud at Home, at School and in the Community*. Ontario: Pembroke Publishers/Heinemann Educational Books.

Bruner, J. (1986) *Actual Minds, Possible Worlds*. Cambridge, Mass.: Harvard University Press.

Colwell, E. (1980) *Storytelling*. London: Bodley Head.

Colwell, Eileen (1991) *Storytelling*. Stroud: The Thimble Press.

Evans, Janet (Ed.) (1998) *What's in the Picture? Responding to illustrations in Picture Books*. London: Paul Chapman Publishing Ltd.

Fox, Carol (1993) *At the Very Edge of the Forest: the Influence of Literature on Storytelling by Children*. London: Cassell.

Garvie, Edie (1990) *Story as Vehicle: Teaching English to Young Children*. Clevedon: Multilingual Matters.

Grainger, Teresa (1997) *Traditional Storytelling in the Primary Classroom*. Leamington Spa: Scholastic.

Gregory, Eve (1996) *Making Sense of a New World: Learning to Read in a Second Language*. London: Paul Chapman Publishing.

Hallworth, Grace (1984) *Mouth Open, Story Jump Out*, London: Methuen.

Heywood, Simon (1998) *The New Storytelling*. Reading: Daylight Press.

Howe, Alan and Johnson, John (eds) (1992) *Common Bonds: Storytelling in the Classroom*. London: Hodder & Stoughton.

Jennings, Claire (1991) *Children as Story-tellers: Developing Language Skills in the Classroom*. Melbourne: Oxford University Press.

Medlicott, Mary (1991) *Time for Telling*. London: Kingfisher Books.

Meek, Margaret (ed.) (1996) *Developing Pedagogies in the Multilingual Classroom: the Writings of Josie Levine*. Stoke-on-Trent: Trentham Books.

Rosen, Betty (1988) *And None Of It Was Nonsense: the Power of Storytelling in School*. London: Mary Glasgow Publications.

Rosen, Betty (1991) *Shapers and Polishers: Teachers as Storytellers.* London : Mary Glasgow Publications.

Wells, G. (1987) The Meaning Makers: Children Learning and Using Language to Learn. London: Hodder & Stroughton.

CHAPTER 3

Teachers and pupils learn the art of storytelling

This chapter draws on case-study material provided by teachers, trainee teachers and their pupils who were working with storytelling in school for the first time. Their stories tell of novices tentatively responding to the climate of enthusiasm, illustrated in the previous chapter, that had been created by the National Oracy Project and endorsed by the National Curriculum. In the 1990s teachers were becoming increasingly aware of research suggesting that the stories heard by children before they enter school have a profound effect on their language and literacy development (Wells 1987) and also that much of the language experience that children bring into school from family and community is in the form of stories that have been told and read to them. Carol Fox's study of stories told by preschool children illustrated the importance of these resources which provide both 'narrative techniques … absorbed from the experiences of hearing written language' and the syntax necessary for complex thinking (Fox 1993:116). There was seen to be a strong link also with learning to read; hearing stories read to them and sharing books with adults was shown to be the best predictor of children's subsequent experience of learning to read (Wells 1987). The structure of the stories that children hear, and often retell, clearly help them to anticipate the way stories work as they learn to read. Hence, the emphasis on storytelling in the National Literacy Strategy (DfEE 1998).

Becoming storytellers

The following account is based on the experience of a number of teachers and trainee teachers who were introducing storytelling with different age groups. As they describe and reflect on different aspects of their experience we can learn a lot about the effectiveness of a variety of strategies that are available to us. And we gather much information about what these experiences offered to the children who encountered them.

Sarah's Story

We start with a teacher, Sarah, as she plans to embark on a term of storytelling with a Year 1 class. She begins with her reasons for wanting to do this:

> I chose to look at the impact of storytelling in a Year 1 classroom for a variety of reasons. As a young child I had a Turkish grandmother who would entertain us with traditional folk tales. I remember listening to her, enthralled by the way she told stories without a book. The stories became very real and alive, different characters had their own distinctive voices and I felt as if I was in the middle of the tale, being fully involved in the action. Remembering the joy I felt listening to these stories, I wanted to pass on this feeling to others. I wanted to show the children that stories do not just come from books but from inside us too. Storytelling is a unique way of bringing people together. When you tell a story you share part of yourself with your audience and I wanted to bring this sense of unity and intimacy into the classroom.
> (Cumming 1998)

Planning and preparation for storytelling

Sarah had not tried this before and planned initially to give every child in her class of twenty-one children the opportunity to tell a story during the course of one term. A time that had previously been given up to listening to stories being read aloud would now be devoted to telling and sharing oral stories:

> The storytime sessions will be concerned with introducing the children to different types of oral stories, retellings of familiar tales, traditional stories from around the world, personal and family stories and invented stories. During each of the storytime sessions the children will be encouraged to listen carefully and then tell their own related stories. So the children will be learning to listen and through this, learning how to construct their own stories. The children's stories will consist of whole-class, group and individual stories. Whole-class stories are where the children suggest characters, significant events, places and items and how the story should be constructed, these suggestions can be incorporated into a story which

the children will be encouraged to retell. Similarly, group stories will allow the children to retell and also later to write their own stories. (Cumming 1998)

She devised a number of strategies and props to support these sessions.

The story apron

The purpose of using aids is to involve the children further in the stories and to help them in the telling of their own stories. One of the aids I will use is the 'story apron'. This will have several large pockets in which items relating to the story being told are kept and these will be produced from the pockets at appropriate moments to bring further interest to the story. The story apron will also be used to signify that storytelling is in progress: only the apron wearer speaks. The children will be encouraged to use the apron and choose their own items for the pockets.

Many teachers use props of this kind to illustrate a story and also adopt various means to give status to the child who is telling the story; sometimes by having a special chair or by holding a particular object to denote the right to speak or, as in this case, by wearing a special garment. Sarah also intended that the props she provided would help the teller to remember the content and sequence of the story:

The props can be used as memory aids where the children relate a particular part of the story to each object, for example 'The Frog Prince' can be broken down into the golden ball part, the pillow part and the crown part. This will also help to develop a greater understanding of story structure, beginning, middle and end.

She also adapted an idea that is mentioned in Teresa Grainger's *Traditional Storytelling* (1997) where a number of strategies which will encourage awareness of story structure are discussed (1997:64). Sarah describes how she intends to use a story plate to identify the key points of a story.

Story plates

This idea will be introduced to the children through a retelling of the story of the willow-pattern plate, the tale of two young lovers who were transformed into birds through the power of their love. I will show the children how the key characters and events of the story are portrayed on the plate. The children will choose a favourite story and identify the key points of the story. They will then decide how to portray these points and illustrate their own plates. These plates can then be used as reference points for the children when they are telling their stories. I am keen to show the children that in storytelling it is the bones of the story that are important but they can flesh out their stories in different ways and it does not have to be exactly the same every time you tell it.

A storytelling cottage

Sarah was also aware that not all children would feel confident enough to tell stories publicly to the whole class and so hit upon the idea of a storytelling 'cottage' where children could go to tape their own tales alone or with friends. These tales would then be available for the children to listen to 'on their very own class story tape'. Setting up a comfortable corner with a tape recorder where children can be alone or with a partner was a strategy often recommended by teachers taking part in the National Oracy Project. Children would be encouraged to respect this space, be it a corner of the classroom or an existing play house and abide by rules drawn up by the whole class, making it clear how many people could use the tape recorder at any time and for how long. This was an idea often used successfully by my students. One told me 'in the storytelling corner I set up, I had two tape recorders, one with blank tapes and one with tapes to be listened to. This corner was used every minute of the day, the children were so prolific with their stories' (Val 1990).

Recording and assessing progress

Sarah intended to monitor the children's progress throughout the project, recording evidence of the development of their literary and language skills, their growing understanding of story structure, character and setting and their imaginative use of language. And, significantly, she wanted to assess 'how far their confidence when speaking in front of an audience increases, how far they develop the use of tone to convey expression, their use of gesture, basically the ways in which they make stories come alive for their audience'. She was also interested, for her own sake, to observe and record, 'what influences children's stories, other stories and books, nursery rhymes, television and how these influences affect the structure, characters and themes of their stories'.

Starting the project

With carefully planned sessions, a range and variety of texts and related activities, Sarah embarked on her project and told her first story of the term.

> I told the children that I was going to tell them a story without using a book. I explained that I had not made up the story but was telling it from memory. As I started all the children sat forward, listening intently. There was no need for me stop telling the story at any point because there were no interruptions – no one talked or wriggled. After I had finished I asked the children if they had enjoyed the story and they all shouted 'Yes!' One child thought that he would be able to tell his own story to the class and I explained that this opportunity would be open to them all ... I was very pleased with this session, the reaction of the children was much more than I could have imagined. They became very involved in the story and focused their listening more than when they have had a story read to them. Having a class of five year olds sit perfectly still, wrapped up in a story, is something I have not seen to this extent before.

Development

After this successful start Sarah's class began to provide real evidence of the impact of storytelling. Each child had the opportunity in the first instance to tell a story to the whole class and even in these early stages, Sarah was able to observe how they grew in confidence and how they influenced each other.

> It was apparent in the storytelling sessions that the children adapted easily to this new experience. Many children were keen to tell their stories from the start while those who were less eager grew quickly in confidence over the weeks, although there were some children who still felt uncomfortable about sharing their stories in public.

These were the children who needed the story cottage or a partner to talk to. For the rest, Sarah felt that there had been impressive developments: 'It became apparent in these sessions that the children did have some clear ideas on story, on structure and on content'.

Factors influencing the children's storytelling

Sarah felt that she was able to see where the stories came from, what was influencing them, and she noticed a developing sense of audience in their use of different strategies as the weeks progressed and the tellers learnt from each other.

Even though the children only had the opportunity to tell just one story, the potential for learning through storytelling was evident. By listening to the tales told by their peers the children seemed to learn about what makes a good story. For example, in the second session, Sarah noticed that they began to use conventional story openings such as 'Once upon a time' and that all subsequent stories started in this way. 'It was as if the children had forgotten about this aspect of storytelling but needed one reminder in order to use it in their own stories'.

A sense of audience

During the storytelling sessions Sarah noticed the value of children listening to stories told by their peers:

> The children were aware that they were entertaining each other and on some occasions it seemed that they were trying to make their stories more exciting than the previous tale heard by the class. A few of them took this sense of audience further. One child used different voices for each character while another used comedy. Many of the stories had children from the class as major characters, in some of the stories all the children were included.

Other students and teachers I have worked with have also noticed the sophisticated way in which quite young children have a sense of audience and seem to know how to enhance their telling by use of intonation, accent and gesture.

Like Sarah, many were surprised by the skill and confidence that emerged when children were allowed to tell their own stories.

Children telling stories

Sue, working in a Milton Keynes First School, recalled that 'It was the most unlikely people who displayed the most unsuspected linguistic resources and strategies'. A quiet boy who 'would often just nod in response to the register and never participated in class discussion' one day whispered to her that he had a story to tell and began 'Once upon a time in a country not far from Milton Keynes lived a little kitten called Tootsy', revealing a hitherto hidden ability to organise language and tell an elaborate story (Grugeon 1998:54). Jane, working with older children in a Cambridgeshire school, discovered equally unexpected talent when an eight year old girl in her class told a powerful ghost story. It seemed that she was already a polished story teller,

> using techniques of pause, different voices, varying dynamic and intonation, to create the type of breathless tension that holds a listener's attention. It was as though she was actually listening to someone else doing the telling, listening with an inner ear that directly informs the brain.
> (Grugeon 1998:57)

She told Jane that her aunt had told her the story and indeed, came to lunch at weekends and regularly told stories. When Jane asked how she remembered them she said, 'I read them out of my head' (Grugeon 1998: 57).

The importance of an audience, the social nature of storytelling, was remarked on by several of the students. Sue noted that in her class,

> the general standard of storytelling was constantly improving. Many of the children were incorporating facial expressions, speech and voice intonation into their developing stories. I was aware that this was actually being acknowledged by the children themselves. Many showing delight at listening to those they enjoyed and listened patiently and respectfully to those they did not.

Vicky tells a similar story of the children's growing confidence: 'the children I asked to tell stories were five to seven year olds and had never been asked to tell stories before. In spite of this, they were not reticent but rather impatient for their turn to come'. Listening to her recordings, Vicky felt that 'different types of story demanded different types of telling'. Two boys sharing a recollection of their trip to America 'required an almost conversational dialogue in which one made a statement and asked for the other's affirmation of the detail'. Another pair of boys had told a fast-moving adventure story,

> The content of the story was fast moving in itself but the boys' voices became very animated as their enthusiasm and personal involvement increased. In places of highest excitement they alternated between teller and listener extremely quickly and with great skill. Their concentration on the story was so powerful that they were both totally caught up in the adventure.

In contrast, two girls in Vicky's class were 'much more sedate in their pace', as they shared the retelling of *Little Red Riding Hood*. 'Their close attention to detail slowed down the tempo as they strove to find the correct sequence of events and even dialogue', but at the same time they 'used their voices to great effect', paying attention to intonation and the rhythm of the words'. Vicky was surprised to discover such awareness and confident use of different storytelling techniques in these young children. Another child had created her own style for a retelling of *The Three Little Pigs*. She did not attempt to produce a correct version but adapted the story in her own way. Vicky describes how:

> The brightness of her voice and enthusiasm for the story drew me and the entire class into a world of straw houses and puffing wolves.
> '"Can I have some of your sticks?"
> "You can have as much as you like."
> So he took 'em all.'
> And when the class laughed at this point, she repeated the phrase in subsequent episodes, reacting to her audience as an experienced storyteller would. This was all the more remarkable since she was considered a less able child.
> (Grugeon 1998:56)

Indeed, some children seemed to have an amazing command of technique. Jane writes about a seven year old:

> His tale was fascinating, the story of a little boy who finds himself, having gone through a small door in a cave, entering a quite different world on the other side, a world of monsters. It was apparent that he was using visual clues to help provide details; for example, 'there was a monster school with monster chairs' (looking at the chairs) 'and monster music' (looking at the music stands). It was equally apparent that he was transforming what he actually saw into some kind of visual imagery, and that he could transmit such images to his audience. An interesting aspect of Toby's story was the monster teacher who spoke monster speak and whom the little boy could not understand. I asked whether the boy ever managed to understand, to which Toby replied 'No, never.' I was left to wonder whether there was an implicit message in this story. Bruner (1986:64) says that 'the young child seems not only to negotiate sense in his exchanges with others but to carry the problems raised by such ambiguities back into the privacy of his own monologues'. Toby's command of devices to convey meanings and atmosphere and his grasp of the conventions of story grammar were impressive for a child of seven years old. Perhaps the most linguistically mature aspect was the ending – 'It had all been a dream'.
> (Grugeon 1998:56)

The influence of stories that children already know

Sarah found that despite a diet of traditional tales being provided in the classroom, and a great deal of evidence that the children's stories were influenced by the tales they had been told, many of them relied heavily on their experience of television: 'The main characters in their stories were from cartoon shows and many of the plots were recognisable as episodes of these cartoons'. She felt that since television is so visual and there is no need for accounts of what places and people look like, children often had little description of character and setting in their stories. However, this may well have been something to do with it being their first experience of telling stories and that they felt safer using a familiar format. Sarah noticed that the stories told during one session often reflected aspects of each other: 'After the first story was told and the children saw a favourable response from the audience they adopted a similar format; this way they were using something they knew had worked instead of putting their confidence on the line by using a format they were unsure of.'

In fact, it seems possible that older children may be able to use TV models to their advantage. Vikki Slater, who was working with seven to nine year old children, also recognised the influence of television but found that, rather than limiting their storytelling development, it might well enhance it.

> During the storytelling sessions, three story influences became apparent. These were, television and film, books and each other's stories. For instance, Ella often used sound effects and American accents in hers that resembled television cartoons. Other children told stories based on animated videos, such as *Peter Pan* and *Snow White*. The latter was very interesting in the sense that it was so obviously influenced by the film. When Rhian was telling it, I could see her visualising the story. Her story shows this through the use of visual images, 'she was so skinny and bony' and 'he's ugly and horrible and he's got these gigantic ears'. She also uses sound effects and American voices and intonation that appear in the film, as well as the song, 'I'm wishing, I'm wishing for wonders all'. At this point, Ella also joins in, as she does on several occasions. On one occasion she also challenges Rhian's retelling with the comment, 'You never said how she went to the house'. This reveals the shared culture of film and television that these children have and use in their stories and on the playground in their role play activities.
> (Slater 1995)

Vikki's evidence suggests that these older children are also significantly influenced by the written word. In a retelling of Rumpelstiltskin, Rhian frequently uses phrases such as 'then all of a sudden', 'in the break of day' and 'one day before the story ended'. This consciously structured language is the 'book language' that the National Literacy Strategy stresses that children must acquire in order to become competent writers (DfEE 1998). Vikki also draws attention to the social nature of storytelling in the way that children influence each other's story content by sharing ideas and often interrupting:

Craig: she was Dracula's wife and his dad was
Ella: Dracula
Craig: No his dad was Frankenstein.
(Slater 1995)

Does the art of storytelling come naturally?

My account of storytelling so far, may have seemed to suggest that it is an art latent in all of us, something that comes naturally, is unproblematic and spontaneous. This may seem to be the case when we read the enthusiastic accounts received from students and teachers above. And it has been asserted in many ways by the writers referred to in Chapter 2 that narrative is part of a powerful human drive to make sense of experience. Barbara Hardy's now well-known and still powerful proposition that narrative is 'to be regarded as a primary act of mind' and her assertion that 'we dream in narrative, daydream in narrative, remember, anticipate, hope, despair, believe, doubt, plan, revise, criticise, construct, gossip, learn, hate and love by narrative ...' (Hardy 1977) has contributed to a belief that we are naturally gifted storytellers. This is evidently not the case. Many of us as adults feel a strong reluctance to tell stories to an audience in a formal situation, which is why we go to great lengths to prepare ourselves for, say, taking assembly. Telling stories is an art which we have to acquire, practise and polish.

Children learning to tell stories

Peter Hollindale reasserts a generally held belief when he claims that 'we construct our selfhood through memory; that we depend for our identity on our sense of personal continuity in time, and that we express this to our selves by storying our lives ... we need stories as we need food, and we need stories most of all in childhood as we need food then, in order to grow'. (Hollindale 1997:70) However, such an assertion naturalises narrative and storytelling and can lead to a belief that there is little for teachers to do other than provide the appropriate stimulus and context and the children will be able to tell stories confidently. It is easy to assume that all children have had some experience of stories before school but even if this were the case, we cannot take it for granted that this experience is evenly distributed across the population; we cannot take it for granted that all children will be able to transfer home learning to the school setting and be able to tell stories or cope with narrative structures easily and spontaneously. Research carried out over a year in a nursery classroom where the children were not familiar with story and did not find it easy to structure a narrative retelling has shown the sensitive skill and understanding required by the teacher as she involved the class in narrative 'to such effect that by the summer months they are capable of sustained and coherent re-tellings of stories they have heard' (Dombey 1992:2). In the process, Dombey describes how they learn a number of complex lessons about narrative which are relevant to their future as readers.

Complex lessons

Students too, involved in introducing storytelling to a class, have often found that they needed to work very hard with children who did not find telling stories easy. Jane reflected on children in her class who had needed help; she drew on her reading of Jerome Bruner and Gordon Wells to help explain why this might be the case: 'I noticed that the child managed the opening and the beginning of the sequence very well but he became confused about how to describe his actual holiday experiences. In fact, this is no easy task since the capacity to construct stories from experience requires, a "natural organisation of mind, one into which we grow through experience rather than one we achieve through learning"' (Jane quoting Bruner 1986:63). Gordon Wells' *The Meaning Makers* offered her a plausible explanation for another child's difficulty in constructing a sequence of events from memory. Wells suggests that, 'making sense of an experience is to a very great extent being able to construct a plausible story about it' (Wells 1987:196). Jane wondered whether the child was unable to construct a story because she could not make sense of her experience or vice versa. She reflected that in either case she would need plenty of talking and reflecting to help her 'through conscious exploration of memory to internalise the meaning of her experiences'.

Wendy recorded a story told by a four year old as he was drawing a picture; on first hearing, a fairly inconsequential monologue which accompanies his actions:

John: Now the elephant is on the ground.

Now he's changed to green

And when he was on the ground he changed to green.

When the chameleon is on the floor it changed to green

When it's on the floor this chameleon

When, when the elephant is on the floor it changes.

Mrs Smith, when the elephant is on the floor it changes green like a chameleon.

Donna: No, it doesn't!

John: It does 'cos it's a magic elephant.

There is the chimney and the smoke is coming out

And it's nearly going to fall on the elephant,

A changing elephant and when it's on the floor it changes yellow.

Donna: Oh!

John: I don't know what this is going to change into.

While this monologue might not seem to be much of a story, Wendy felt that John was developing the beginnings of a narrative structure and content. She knew where it was coming from, 'John has created an elaborate story around the previous week's tale of *The Mixed Up Chameleon*, this week's folk tale of *The Elephant and the Rabbit* about an elephant who changes his appearance' and a local event when some chimney stacks had been demolished, which the whole class had seen on TV and talked about. In combining real and fantasy events, Wendy felt that he had begun to create a 'possible world' into which Donna, his audience, was beginning to be drawn. Already, at the age of four, he reveals his dependence on stories that he had heard and read before. In recording the stories that their children told, many of the students that I was working with were discovering that, 'any story presupposes the existence of other stories … for both reader and listener threads of connection exist, threads of many different kinds' (Rosen 1984:33). Most of the stories that they recorded bore out Carol Fox's finding in her own study that, 'The model for the children's stories was very obviously literary' (Fox 1993:97). Understanding the intertextual nature of all stories helps us to recognise what is influencing tentative attempts like John's and to consider ways in which we can help children to begin to turn a random monologue which may accompany their play or drawing, into a consciously shaped story.

Starting with our own stories

Models do not necessarily have to be literary; they may be based on personal anecdote. Working with a Year 2 class of six and seven year olds

Kathryn had told a story about herself, 'When I was a little girl …'. Her story about a childhood incident involving a wet swimming costume modelled the kind of story that she hoped they would be able to tell. She felt that she was offering a safe starting point and structure. At first, she felt that the children's stories were fairly thin. For example, Fred's tentative response, 'Once when I was little and on the climbing frame there was lots of webs and I saw a spider one and I scared it and it fell off its web by saying "boo"'. While it has an embryonic story structure it also suggests that Fred is stuck when it comes to creating a more elaborate story based on his own experience. He is much more confident when he is retelling a familiar tale: 'Mother Pig said "You've grown too much for this house. You'd better build a house of your own"'. He confidently uses phrases which echo versions that he has heard before, 'The wolf came along and he brought the house down', 'The third little pig decided to build a house with a strong brick wall', 'He fell in with a splash and that was the last of him'. The language of the familiar tale scaffolds his telling; the story based on his own experience has no such support.

However, Milly, in the same class, can tell an elaborate personal story and it seems that she is drawing on previous experience of storytelling. It may be a story that has been told many times in her own family as she confidently uses narrative conventions of repetition and dialogue to create effect:

> Once I was little and I was only about one. My mummy put my nappy on and said 'stay there for a minute' … and I took my nappy off and ran away and hid and I said, 'no mummy not going to take my nappy off … don't take nappy off'. So I ran and then mummy caught me and put my nappy on again, so I took it off and ran away again and mummy said 'don't do that again' and she put my nappy on again and I took it off and ran away again and this time I hid under the bed ….
> (Stone 1999)

We can sense from this extract that Milly is really enjoying the story and responding to laughter from her audience, as she continues to remove her nappy (now fastened with 'three big pieces of sellotape') and find different hiding places until the story reaches a splendid climax with her mother triumphant at last, 'that's why I asked you to keep your nappy on!' While this elaborate account of a personal experience seems to be unique to Milly, we can see that it draws heavily on conventions learnt from the stories that she is hearing and reading. The process of hearing, telling and retelling is adding to her skill as a storyteller. This was no less the case for her teacher who felt that during the time that she spent introducing her class to storytelling she too was acquiring new skills:

For me the requirement to model the storytelling exercises meant that my confidence as an effective storyteller has improved. In addition to recalling storylines or creating new stories instantaneously, I also developed certain traits which enhanced my storytelling, such as momentous pauses, vocal changes and maintaining eye contact with all members of the audience.

(Stone 1999)

Teaching and learning storytelling techniques

As we have discussed above, storytelling as an art form does not come naturally, but the impulse to tell stories is in all of us and with careful encouragement can be enhanced. In the primary school many teachers believe in this kind of encouragement. Emma Lazenby, working in a large multi-cultural school with a group of mixed ability Year 2 children, many of whom had English as an additional language, wanted to see whether she could improve the children's competence as storytellers. Using as her starting point Fiona French's retelling of *Anancy and Mr Dry-Bone* (1991), she tried a number of strategies suggested by Jennings (1991) and Grainger (1997) to improve technique and presentation over a period of weeks. Step by step the children worked towards a whole-class presentation. At first the children worked individually, then in pairs, then in larger groups, using story maps and puppets. Slowly, Emma could see them developing a sense of audience and a heightened awareness of the language they used. Looking at Eisha over a six week period she noted considerable development. In her retelling of the story at the individual level she noted that 'her tale was monotonous and simply recalled information'; however, once she was working with a partner there were developments, she was beginning to adopt a range of voices for the characters and was 'using other strategies in order to make her story more enjoyable to the listener … using more expression and intonation' and the story seemed less disjointed. 'During the group sessions, Eisha made considerable developments in the way she drew upon many strategies for telling her story in order to maximise the dramatic effect on her listeners.' She used a range of intonation patterns, voices for characters and even began to use dramatic pauses, 'And then … there was a knock at the door and there was Mr Dry-Bone'. After the first two sessions, Emma observed that 'she became more aware of the characters involved, the setting and the plot. Her ability to pick out the main points of the story and to give emphasis to the structure also improved' (Lazenby 1999). This had also been enhanced by Emma's use of puppets, story maps and ladders with the whole class to aid the children's understanding of the characters, setting and the plot. The other children all made similar progress. The weeks Emma had spent slowly building up confidence and concentrating on technique had paid off. The children's competence as storytellers had shown impressive development. By concentrating on the retelling of only one story, reworking it from week to week, Emma had made them aware of a range of strategies; they had moved on from a simple retelling of the content to a re-creation of the story in a number of animated versions which paid attention to the response of an audience.

Working with older children

It would seem likely that as children grow older and more experienced and are enjoying a wider range of narratives at home and at school, they will inevitably become more confident and competent storytellers. However, it appears that storytelling tends to be seen as important at a preliterate stage and becomes less significant as story reading and writing take over.

Despite support from the National Curriculum and the National Literacy Strategy for the inclusion of storytelling and continuing encouragement to develop children's awareness of narrative techniques at Key Stage 2, the focus is more on writing, especially with older children. Storytelling at Key Stage 2 is no less important than at an earlier stage, yet may be less in evidence. A professional storyteller, involved in research into the oral narratives of teenagers, described the scepticism that he encounters among teachers about the existence of a significant narrative tradition belonging to older children and the value of storytelling for them. His experience of working with adolescents to compile an archive of 'riddles, ghost stories, family lore, contemporary legends, local legends, creation myths, jocular tales, superstitions and personal experience stories' seems to contradict this (Wilson 1994:3). Since it is unlikely that the examples he is collecting appear suddenly when children transfer to secondary school, it is possible that there is a developing narrative tradition unnoticed on the playground, and out of school, throughout the primary school years. Certainly this seemed to be the case when Vikki Slater recorded stories and jokes in the school playground and at summer play schemes. She found much evidence of role-play games based on television, film and computer games. In 1995 she observed 'television programmes such as *Superman*, *Power Rangers* and *Eladoir* seemed to have a major influence, as well as cartoons like *Paratroopers*, *Reeboot* and *Top Cat* that they watched on satellite television'. In 1995 *The Lion King* was the film that most influenced role-play games. The range of programmes would be similar but possibly even wider in 2000. The influence of computer games was also much in evidence with many references to *Sonic the Hedgehog*, *Lemmings* and *Jurassic Park*; whatever is currently popular will almost certainly have taken on this role. At the time of writing, it seems likely that the influence of adult cartoons on TV, like *South Park* will very probably be evident in children's games and their writing. In the classroom the challenge, particularly with older children, is to find stories that will offer the same degree of excitement and satisfaction.

Retelling stories: the power of traditional tales

Encouraging the art of storytelling from Year 5 to Year 8 needs detailed and informed preparation. This is modelled beautifully in a video recording of a Year 6 class preparing to tell stories to the infant class during the school's book week (Aylwin and Peters 1989). At first the whole class hears and retells a number of traditional tales that they have never heard before. They take it in turns to work at an initial retelling, sitting in a large circle and passing the story on from one to the next; the teller who has joined the class teacher for this project sits in the circle prompting and nudging the story along. Next they take part in a workshop: pairs take on the story that they are going to tell, practising telling and retelling, polishing and improving with the teacher and storyteller commenting on and discussing their technique, building their confidence until they are ready to perform their stories in front of an audience. At regular intervals they come together in larger groups and listen to each other commenting critically, putting forward better means of creating effects: one group works to help a particular boy try out different ways to create the voice of the wind in his story. They try out a number of ideas until all are satisfied that he is achieving the best effect. They make suggestions about gesture, eye contact and pace, constantly returning to the needs of the audience. Working in pairs they have a partner to share the story, to prompt and support them during the telling. When they finally tell their tales, they sit on a decorated, throne-like chair. The whole event has taken considerable preparation and becomes a high-status performance.

This video was based on the work of Tony Aylwin at the University of Greenwich which has a long tradition of storytelling in teacher education. In a brief account of this project, he discusses the interesting differences that he noticed between the written versions that the children heard and their own oral versions. The children often make changes which bring the stories closer to the experience of their audience, combining the more formal language of the story with the dialect that they share with their audience, helping 'to make the story more effective for the young audience' (Aylwin 1992:51-2). He illustrates the way this was taking place by comparing the beginning of one of the stories that the children were working with, a version of a tale from the Arabian Nights, with a version told by one of the children:

> From the far side of the desert comes the story – though who can tell if it is true – of an unremarkable town full of unremarkable people. Among them lived a little beggar, remarkable for his smallness of size. He was such pleasant company that townsfolk would often ask him home to dinner.
> (McCaughrean, G., quoted in Aylwin 1992)

Aylwin then comments on Amy's version 'devised and rehearsed during the workshop practices ... the beggar becomes a boy who lives in London though the time is still appropriately in the distant past':

> Years ago, ages and ages ago, there was a little boy and he was a beggar boy. Nobody knew his name or where he'd come from but he lived in a little village in London ... Er, in those days London wasn't a big city like it is now. It was just broken down old little huts, so the beggar lived in one of the alleyways and everybody used to ask him round for dinner ... because in return they would get a story from the beggar. The beggar was a brilliant storyteller.
> (Aylwin 1992)

He comments that when Amy retells this well-prepared story she uses a range of paralinguistic features and suggests that:

> As with the development of literacy skills, the key to making children sensitive to story telling skills in their mixture of formal and informal language and variety of 'voices', seems to lie in providing real audiences for them to interact with.
> (Aylwin 1992)

The meticulous preparation of teachers at Greenwich, who were going to introduce storytelling in school, provided a model for other institutions. From 1990 onwards it became part of the programme at De Montfort University and students who were going into junior and middle schools, as well as those working with younger classes, were encouraged to give storytelling a try.

Planning, preparation and confidence building

Many of the students at that time greeted the idea of becoming storytellers with less than warm enthusiasm, 'I was filled with horror and panic, I had never told a story before' and tended to believe that storytelling was an inappropriate activity for young children (Grugeon1992). They clearly needed to feel more comfortable with the idea and to build up their own repertoire and skills. We used techniques we had learnt from Betty Rosen, Mary Medlicott and Tony Aylwin to prepare them before they went into schools. In these sessions they were to spend much more time telling stories to each other and developing strategies for getting storytelling off the ground. We used ideas from the National Oracy Project and the Channel 4 TV *Word of Mouth* series. These were excellent programmes which introduced professional storytellers from a number of different cultures telling tales to adults. This not only extended the students' repertoire of traditional yarns which would be more appropriate for older children but also introduced them to 'state of the art' practitioners. It was accompanied by excellent notes with written versions of the stories told and articles on the theory and practice of telling tales. It made a very useful contribution to raising the status of storytelling.

The students were involved in workshop sessions in which they tried out activities for use in school. One of these was Mary Medlicott's 'Leather Bag': in a circle participants pass a real or imaginary bag from one person to the next while chanting in unison:

'Here is a grand old leather bag, pass it on, pass it on
Into this bag I'm going to put
Something from story, rhyme or song.'

And the person who is holding the bag at that point declares what they are going to put in, such as 'Cinderella's glass slipper' and the refrain is picked up as the bag continues round the circle. The aim is to collect references to traditional tales and for the participants to realise what a wealth of shared reference they have. Another game involves passing a story round a group; each player must start their contribution with either 'fortunately' or 'unfortunately'; this can lead to much hilarity and clever manipulation by participants of the way the story is going. The group then moved on to telling and retelling personal experience stories to each other. Sharing anecdotes proved a good starting point. I have never known a student or child who could resist telling the story of their scar! Or talking about 'the most frightening thing that ever happened to me'.

As well as discovering and developing their own skills, the students had an experience of being in the audience themselves. A local teacher, who was a professional storyteller, came into one of their sessions to introduce them to Anansi the trickster spider from the Caribbean. She talked about the importance of telling traditional tales and building up a personal repertoire of stories from different cultures. As well as making them aware of the potential for using props, magnetic and felt boards, puppets and artefacts relating to the story, she had reminded them how such stories can be a way of exploring real life dilemmas; how they can 'transcend and unite cultures by depicting universal morals and truths' (Gregory 1996:116).

The students also had a second chance to experience a professional storyteller at work.They joined a group of children at a dramatic telling of *The Hairy Toe* by one of the University's drama lecturers. Both storytelling sessions had helped to prepare them for their own storytelling; as one wrote, the first session had made them aware of the importance of 'having at one's fingertips a range of folk tales from many cultures to use in today's multi-ethnic classrooms in order to broaden everyone's horizons'. The second session had provoked thoughts about the way a potentially frightening story might be handled or mediated by the teller. Jane described how she felt that this had happened:

> Firstly, the way the story was told, the 'virtual' nature of the language and the voice, committed the children's minds and senses and secondly, the emotion of fear was kept at bay by inviting them to become involved as participants and partners in the telling.

In this way, she had felt that 'the teller hands over some power and responsibility for the telling and this reduces the emotional fear'; the teller had maintained the listeners' involvement but defused the anxiety. She felt that 'we do not generally fear that which we have power to control', and when she told the story of *The Hairy Toe* herself, she had hoped to defuse further any potential fear by getting children to model, paint and draw the creature the hairy toe had belonged to. In reflecting on the children's response to this story, she wondered about the effect of such a 'powerful genre' and suggested that these stories were using what Bruner has called the 'language of consciousness' (Bruner 1986) and felt that this 'could have profound implications for the way in which children use language to express their view of the world'. She speculated that, 'as Carol Fox suggests, "whatever lies at the heart of storytelling lies at the heart of language itself"'(Fox in Meek and Mills 1988:55).

As the students became more confident, they were expected to work in pairs to prepare a story to perform to the whole group. They were encouraged to use props and think of strategies to involve their audience in different ways. In this way they all increased their repertoire of stories and showed each other a range of techniques which involved the use of puppets, pictures, hats, bags, boxes, percussion and musical instruments.

Reflecting on early experiences of telling stories

This detailed preparation paid off and provided useful feedback. One student described how she had used the techniques we had practised to prepare her class for a retelling of 'The Land Where No-one Ever Dies' (Rosen 1988:94-7):

> The session began by discussing what these Year 6 children already knew about storytelling from TV, family members and friends. We then progressed on to the fact that they were all very adept at this art form and practised it frequently – much to their amusement. From this point we moved on to experiences with stories starting from very early memories and moving to present favourites. This revealed to them a very wide repertoire already in stock and produced some brief retellings. To involve everyone fully in the experience we then embarked on 'The Brown Leather Bag' exercise and all contributed 'something from story, rhyme or song.' It was lovely to see the variety of choices and the inhibitions being broken down by involvement in clapping and reciting the rhyme. This progressed on to passing a story round which we had to repeat twice because it was enjoyed so much.
> I then put myself forward as a storyteller and embarked upon my tale. The children listened spellbound for the twenty minutes or so it took to tell. The attention held by the teacher as storyteller was incredible and brought home to me the power that can be held over an audience in such a situation. Oh, if only this was true in all teaching episodes! There was a silence spread over the children at the end of the tale which was broken by one child who said, 'Was that really true?'
> (Frances 1990)

The children then retold the story with talk partners before discussing issues arising from the story itself, 'which bits stood out for individuals, which bits held personal meaning, the role of death in life, attitudes to dying, missing loved ones, the feeling of security at home – the list was endless'. Like many of her peers, Frances had felt apprehensive about telling a story, 'extremely nervous and self-conscious'; however, as the session progressed she says 'I grew in confidence and felt the enjoyment and creative force of storytelling'.

Growing in confidence

If all this sounds too good to be true, a second student who was working with a Year 5 class described an experience which was not such plain sailing:

> I had chosen 'The kingdom under the sea', a short story by Joan Aiken, as it was quite interesting and easy to learn – lots of repetition, recurring use of the number three. I was going to introduce the session with a discussion of what they thought about telling stories and use the rhyme game, 'Here is a grand old leather bag'. I explained what we were going to do and asked them to place their chairs in a circle (something quite new to them); this was accomplished reasonably well and I began the session. The children were, or rather the eight or so 'excitable' ones, rather high, so it was fairly difficult. When I introduced the clapping rhythm for my rhyme, pandemonium ensued and I had to abandon it to save my credibility. When they were reseated and had remained silent for a while, I introduced the fortunately/unfortunately game as I didn't feel the few should spoil it for the others who were obviously disappointed. This went really well and the story was enjoyed by all. Everybody participated. I was determined to try this again and was able to do so in the following week and having explained the idea of a talking partner, I began with the story. It was wonderful to watch their faces. I really warmed to my task and enjoyed myself. The children worked well with their partners, in general, although some didn't want to work together at first as they were not used to working collaboratively. With more practice I hope this wouldn't be a consideration. Even so, we managed to reconstruct the story. If someone missed out a section then someone else would fill in the missing bit. I thought afterwards what a good and painless way this would be to assess speaking and listening skills – choosing a group to retell the story.
>
> (Ann 1990)

In junior and middle schools many had found it more difficult to fit storytelling into the time allocated to English. This is more likely to be the case in future as the specific demands of the Literacy and Numeracy Strategies make planning very tight. However, it is possible to develop storytelling in other curriculum areas, as you will read in Chapter 4. Certainly, students found many imaginative ways to develop the skill of storytelling outside the time allocated to English. Ongoing projects or topics in schools would often provide scope for telling yarns. In one school the children had seen a TV programme on the Middle Ages; working in groups they taped joint stories which told the story from the point of view of one of the characters. In another school, Year 6 was working on 'Space'; the student completed the topic with storytelling, using an overhead projector to tell the tale of Orion. The children were then helped to make props to tell their own stories to the class, 'the children were thoroughly engrossed and their stories, which I recorded, made the whole experience worthwhile'. Another student, in the same school, got her class to make up science fiction stories; they worked in groups to tell their own tales, complete with sound effects, on tape.

Reflections on becoming storytellers

In this chapter, we have heard the voices of students and children who are experiencing storytelling for the first time. We have seen how teachers and students in training have been able to overcome their initial misgivings about telling stories and become experienced practitioners, providing confident models for the children they were working with. Vicky reflected on her early experience when, 'the story began rather shakily, probably due to my inexperience and slight apprehension at holding thirty children's attention with my voice'. As the children began to join in and take over a story that they already knew her confidence increased. Belinda felt that the children had confirmed her belief that stories could be a 'vehicle to understanding yet an end in themselves ... The intimate and mutually enjoyable nature of storytelling helped to build trusting, positive relationships which formed a secure base from which to explore ideas.' Sue recognised that she could now develop aspects of storytelling and would be more confident about bringing the children into the stories by means of song, repetitive phrases and drama. She saw the value of encouraging a wider exchange of stories and was able to suggest ways of doing this: by inviting older children, parents and professional storytellers into the classroom:

> I also think that it is important to include stories from different cultures, and where appropriate, in a variety of languages. This would expand the children's experiences of different cultures, promoting and nurturing positive attitudes towards other languages and cultural backgrounds.
> (Grugeon 1998:59)

Wendy was able to take this further and reflect on its significance.

> by demonstrating that oral storytelling is very important in school we are saying to children that stories have value. By holding in esteem

the children's own stories and those of their family or culture we are saying that we hold them and their culture in esteem. Children are very new to the difficult task of reading and writing and for many years after starting school are more likely to be able to express themselves fluently and accurately orally. Giving high esteem to oracy gives children a chance to do well and feel good about themselves long before they have become literate.
(Grugeon 1998:59)

Conclusion: mastering the art of storytelling

Between 1990 and 1999 many teachers and students had also begun to discover the impressive range of skills and versatility in their stories as children create, reshape and interpret their experience. They had found latent oral narrative skills, both their own and the children's, which they were able to analyse, becoming aware of the means by which a storyteller, in unique ways, is thinking through language. They had also found that narrative was not as easy for children as they had supposed and needed careful planning, intervention and support. They began to discover ways in which storytelling was helping their pupils to shape experience and develop narrative strategies and to see that the models for children's storytelling are predominantly literary. They also noticed that older children were drawing on a wide range of influences, confidently using the rhetorical devices of traditional tales and fiction stories that they were hearing and reading in school and combining these with their own real life experience, peer interaction in the culture of the playground and the shared experience of TV, video and computer games. In developing the art of storytelling they had become more aware of the importance of narrative and oracy in the development of literacy.

References

Aylwin, A. (1992) 'Retelling Stories', in Dombey, H. and Robinson, M. (eds) *Literacy for the 21st Century*. Brighton: The Literacy Centre, Brighton Polytechnic.

Aylwin, A. and Peters, J. (1989) *Children as Storytellers*, video cassette and booklet, Thames Polytechnic.

Bruner, Jerome (1986) *Actual Minds, Possible Worlds*. Cambridge, Mass.: Harvard University Press.

Cumming, Sarah Jane (1998) 'A Study of the Impact of Storytelling on a Year One Class'. Unpublished BEd Dissertation, De Montfort University.

DfEE (1998) *The National Literacy Strategy Framework for Teaching.* London: DfEE.

Dombey, H. (1992) 'Early lessons in reading narrative'. IEDPE Conference Barcelona, Imprime par l'Universite Paris-Nord.

Fox, Carol (1989) 'Children thinking through story', *English in Education* **23** (2), 25-36.

Fox, Carol (1993) *At the Very Edge of the Forest: the Influence of Literature on Storytelling by Children.* London: Cassell.

French, Fiona (1991) *Anancy and Mr. Dry-Bone.* London: Frances Lincoln.

Grainger, Teresa (1997) *Traditional Storytelling in the Primary Classroom*, Leamington Spa: Scholastic.

Gregory, E. (1996) *Making Sense of a New World: Learning to Read in a Second Language.* London: Paul Chapman Publishing.

Grugeon, E. (1992) 'Becoming Storytellers: Working with student teachers', in Dombey, H. and Robinson, M. (eds) *Literacy for the 21st Century.* Brighton: The Literacy Centre Brighton Polytechnic.

Grugeon, E. *et al.* (1998) *Teaching Speaking and Listening in the Primary School.* London: David Fulton.

Hardy, Barbara (1977) 'Towards a poetics of fiction: an approach through Narrative', in Meek M. *et al.* (eds) *The Cool Web.* London: Bodley Head.

Hollindale P. (1997) *Signs of Childness in Children's Books.* Stroud: The Thimble Press.

Jennings, Claire (1991) *Children as Story-tellers: Developing Language Skills in the Classroom.* Melbourne: Oxford Universtiy Press.

Lazenby, Emma (1999) 'An investigation into the benefits of storytelling with a group of children'. Unpublished BEd Dissertation, De Montfort University.

Medlicott, M. (ed.) (1990) *By Word of Mouth: the Revival of Storytelling*, C4 Broadside Publications.

Meek, M. and Mills, C. (eds) (1988) *Language and Literacy in the Primary School.* Lewes: The Falmer Press.

Rosen, Betty (1988) *And None of it was Nonsense: the Power of Storytelling in School.* London: Mary Glasgow Publications.

Rosen, Harold. (1984) *Stories and Meanings.* Sheffield: NATE.

Slater (neé Taylor), Vikki (1995) 'Can children's playground culture contribute to their classroom experience?' Unpublished BEd Dissertation, De Montfort University.

Stone, Kathryn (1999) 'An investigation into whether an increased exposure to the use of props for storytelling enhances children's use of narrative'. Unpublished BEd Dissertation, De Montfort University.

Wells, Gordon (1987) *The Meaning Makers*. London: Hodder & Stoughton.

Wilson, M. (1994) 'Teenagers and oral narrative', *Lore and Learning*. **2** (July 1994).

CHAPTER 4

Story across the curriculum

When the National Curriculum was devised in 1988, alongside the statutory orders for the core and foundations subjects was non-statutory guidance in a number of cross-curricular themes, skills and dimensions. These included such things as Personal, Social and Health Education (PSHE), multicultural education and economic awareness. It was intended that these non-statutory aspects would be mapped onto the statutory elements by individual schools through their long-, medium- and short-term planning. However, the sheer pace at which the statutory aspects of the curriculum were implemented left little time for non-statutory aspects to be mapped comprehensively.

It was not until the recommendations of Sir Ron Dearing (1994), implemented in September 1995, that space was created for schools to re-establish their curriculum priorities. Schools filled the new '20% discretionary time' in different ways. Some, recognising the demands at Key Stages 1 and 2 of the 'basics', gave increased time to Maths and English; others devoted time to PSHE. However, the relaxation of the curriculum was short lived. With the change of government in 1997 fresh initiatives were proposed, linked to specific national targets in literacy (reading) and numeracy. The political imperative to achieve the targets (80 per cent of pupils attaining Level 4 in Reading and 75 per cent attaining Level 4 in Number by 2002) resulted in further curriculum change with the implementation of the National Literacy Framework in September 1998, followed a year later by the National Numeracy Framework. With these two 'blocks' occupying more space in the centre ground of the curriculum, closely surrounded by science, Information and Computer Technology (ICT), Religious Education (RE) and the remaining Attainment Targets of English and mathematics, forming the 'new' core curriculum, not only were the foundation subjects pushed to the outer edges of what increasingly looked like a flat earth curriculum, but the themes and dimensions, even where they had managed to occupy a place in the educational landscape, began to fall off the edge.

However, curriculum change is far from a linear story. It is through the curriculum that a society tries to create an image of itself, its future, as well as its past (Gaine and George 1999:68). The complexities of the modern world; the plurality of cultures, languages and religions; the opportunities provided by the information revolution; the globalisation of world markets and interdependence of nations; together with the threat of global warming and the spectre of inter-ethnic conflict, force us to reflect continually on who we are and where we think we are going. For these reasons, our collective sense of self, the skills, knowledge, under-standings and values deemed essential prerequisites in the grounding education of future citizens in such a world, are continually contested. Each time we hold a mirror to the world we see a slightly different view, perceived through the lens of changing perspectives. With the state school curriculum under much tighter political control than at any point in its history, it is not surprising that changes in the composition of those who make policy result in changes to curriculum content. Early indications of the revised curriculum for the new millennium indicate that new statutory orders will stand firmly on philosophical foundations encapsulated through citizenship, environmental education including sustainable development, spiritual and moral education, PSHE and equal opportunities (QCA 1999a, QCA 1999b). In order to accommodate change in the primary sector, curriculum planning, particularly beyond the core subjects, requires teachers to prioritise, reduce and combine programmes of study in the foundation subjects (QCA 1998).

Irrespective of the particularities of change, effective teachers use a variety of methods, strategies and approaches, making for a complex repertoire of teaching in order to bring their classrooms alive and to capture the interest and imagination of their pupils (Gipps *et al.* 1999). One such strategy that has stood the test of time is story. Through narrative, experience can be re-lived, topics introduced, the past brought into the present and the far-flung made familiar. Narrative can also act as a powerful mnemonic. Through the structure of language learners are able to make connections between otherwise unrelated information which can be held in the memory far longer than information learned as separate items (Cooper and McIntyre 1992, Howe 1999:37). Story, then, is one means by which meaningful contexts for children's learning may be created; the 'scaffold' teachers use to help pupils climb from the known to the unfamiliar and beyond. In this chapter we draw on the experience of several teachers and university colleagues who have used story in different areas of the curriculum. What is evident from these accounts is the tremendous versatility of story as a pedagogic tool.

The chapter is not intended to be a comprehensive overview of the use of story in the curriculum, but is a selective dip into practice. Readers, for their part, may wish to take these models and apply and adapt them, or invent their own, to suit their own curriculum interests.

Since the Education Reform Act of 1988, science has been a central and statutory aspect of the school curriculum. Initially, many teachers had to adapt their teaching practice to include more science than they were used to doing. This raised anxieties about what to teach and more importantly, how to teach it. In the absence of in-service training, there was an unfortunate tendency for primary science teaching to mimic the secondary science teaching that teachers themselves had experienced at school. To counter this tendency, by extending the range of approaches available to teachers, several initiatives were launched. Among them was the Science from Stories Project, funded through the Hertfordshire Teaching Scholarship, with which one of our colleagues at De Montfort University, Marilyn Leask, was involved. Based on an article, originally published in *The Queensland Science Teacher*, 1993 Vol. 198 No. 2, Marilyn discusses some of the issues and recommendations that arose from the project. Her account is followed by the practical experience of another of our colleagues, Barbara Leedham, who recounts how one teacher used the story *Goldilocks and the Three Bears* to instigate scientific investigation with early Key Stage 1 pupils. The teacher, who was not a science specialist, discovered how it was possible to use children's natural curiosity to encourage them to raise questions which could then be turned into a form capable of being investigated. 'Problematic Porridge' provides a useful illustration of the points raised in Marilyn's account.

After considering science, we turn to data handling, part of the mathematics curriculum. Before giving some practical accounts of the way Paul Gardner has used story in PSHE and environmental education we turn to history and geography in the curriculum. John Sampson, Head of the Primary BEd programme at De Montfort, outlines the possibilities as well as the dangers of using story in history, and Georgina Elton, also at De Montfort, considers the place of story for critical geography. In the penultimate section of the chapter another De Montfort colleague, Paul Frecknall, demonstrates the interconnectedness of story and drama. To conclude the chapter we take a very broad definition of the curriculum; one which acknowledges that everything a school communicates to its pupils should be conceptualised as curriculum, including that which might be described as 'hidden' (Barnes 1976). A colleague at Portfields Combined School, Milton Keynes, Carol Smith, who worked briefly with Liz Grugeon as a seconded teacher to the university, shares her anecdotes of 'Cloudy', a larger than life cat who became an integral part of school life. What the Cloudy stories demonstrate, and what sets them apart from our other examples, is the fact that schools evolve lives of their own, beyond the curriculum.

Science from stories for seven year olds

The Science From Stories Project was designed to test the idea of integrating the development of science knowledge and understanding with the whole curriculum. It was also intended that alternative approaches to science teaching, that were beginning to find their way into the teacher's repertoire of skills, should be shared as widely as possible. Among these were the use of drama, poetry and prose, which were being used to develop children's understanding of scientific concepts. It was particularly noted that literature could provide excellent opportunities for developing questioning, prediction, and observation skills where the work is set in contexts familiar to the children. An advantage of using stories in science is that storytelling and story writing are a natural part of the work of the primary school. Their use to stimulate thinking and language development in science is, therefore, a strategy which fits into the normal rhythm of the classroom.

In the early 1990s the use of drama, nursery rhymes and stories to develop work in science was supported by an emerging literature. The 'Science from Stories' booklets produced at the Northamptonshire Science Centre showed how the process skills of observation, prediction, investigation, measuring and communicating could be developed. Another LEA team, Birmingham Curriculum Support Service, produced two useful books – *Science and Technology through Nursery Rhymes* (1993a) and *Science and Technology through Traditional Tales* (1993b). The BBC ran a 'Science Challenge Series' using traditional tales from around the world (Wilkins and McLean 1991). Christofi and Davies (1991) and Howard (1992) describe the use of drama in science and include ideas that are transferable to design technology. Now teachers are using the internet to do joint story and poetry writing with children and teachers in other locations. Such projects can be accessed through the British Council Montage website (http:/www.bc.org.au/montage) and the European School Net Project (http://www.eun.org).

Stories for the older age group were given a boost by the publication of Professor Russell Stannard's works, *The Time and Space of Uncle Albert* (1989) and *Black Holes and Uncle Albert* (1991), which introduce pupils to Einstein's Theory of Relativity. Adults also find them very readable.

The use of stories to pass on knowledge and to develop understanding of the world is a recurrent theme in this book. We have touched on research into the effectiveness of story as a learning strategy but Strube (1990:54) adds that 'A scientific concept turned into a character has the advantage of increased familiarity, in both senses of an often-encountered and more intimate acquaintance'.

By means of an alternative language of science, a language of questioning, discovery and uncertainty, a challenge can be made to the stereotypical image of the white-coated professor (male) working in splendid isolation in the laboratory. Stories enable teachers to steer their pupils away from the narrow notion of there being one correct answer and promote a more open understanding of scientific work. Anecdotal evidence of teachers and my own experience lead me to think that girls in particular enjoy stories while boys show a preference for factual books. If there is some truth in this then it is an additional argument for formalising the science stories approach, to open up a new methodology of science teaching and learning. The equal opportunities dimension of stories in science teaching is further exemplified in the work of Lucy Skoss, a teacher in the Northern Territory, who shows how traditional native stories can be used to develop aboriginal children's understanding of scientific concepts. The key point here is that by embedding concepts in children's known world meaningful contexts for learning are created.

The Science from Stories Project identified a range of formats that were effective. These include:

- Stories in photocopiable format with spaces for recording illustrations of investigative work, or literature-based research.
- Personalised stories in which individual children's names are inserted. Pupils read with added interest when they see they are part of the story. This provides a special incentive for poor readers and the effect can be achieved easily if the story is on disk.
- Wall stories where pupils present different scenes from a story through display.
- Open-ended stories which involve children using their imagination to develop a story. These stories can involve problem solving using familiar situations.
- Illustrated story books.

A more recent development is CD ROM and the use of multimedia presentations by children (Mitra, in Leask and Meadows 2000) to improve children's understanding of science through stories.

'Problematic Porridge'

The teacher is the enabler in the learning environment. She has the task of bringing children into contact with objects and events to study. For young children a scientific investigation is often an extension or progression of their play. Investigations must be activity based, and offer opportunities for children to develop ideas through their interactions with materials, observation and imagination. In keeping with the requirements of the National Curriculum Programme of Study, investigations ought not to be totally predetermined by the teacher. It is vitally important that children are thorougly involved in the decision-making process. They need to have ownership of the task; to be responsible for making choices about what to do, what to use, and how to record their observations or measurements.

It is also important to remember that children cannot be expected to work scientifically without either having previously experienced the investigative process or having a firm grasp of the area of science being studied. When both the concepts involved and the process of investigation are new to them there is too much of a cognitive load for them to cope with. If they are not used to scientific enquiry then both context and content need to be very familiar. A visit to the pantomime *Goldilocks and the Three Bears* brought inspiration to one teacher I encountered as an Advisory Teacher in Buckinghamshire.

I had never given much thought to those words I must have heard Goldilocks say a thousand times over the years, 'Daddy Bear's porridge is too hot. Mummy Bear's porridge is too cold. But Baby Bear's porridge is just right.' In the warmth of the theatre, surrounded by numerous school parties, I suddenly dropped my suspension of disbelief. How could the bowls contain porridge at different temperatures? It was a problem I shared with my pupils the next day. The children agreed with David when he said:

'I think Daddy's and Mummy's porridge will be hotter than Baby Bear's, even when Baby Bear's is just right. They'll have more.'

The question they wanted to answer was: how could Mummy Bear's porridge in the story be colder than Baby Bear's? This was the prompt that was needed to investigate the question scientifically and the children set about the task. Holly wrote a list of what they would need:

porridge, some water, the cooker, a wooden spoon, a thermometer, and three bowls – small, medium and large.

Laura described what they did:

> *We made the porridge. Then, when it was quite hot we poured it into three bowls. Dad had the biggest bowl so he got more and Mum had a fair bit because hers was medium sized. Baby had a small portion as he had a small bowl.*

They tasted Baby Bear's porridge several times and agreed at 60 degrees that it was 'just right'. David explained what happened:

> *This is Joanne trying Baby Bear's porridge to see if it is just right. We tested the temperatures. We tested Baby Bear's first. We put the thermometer in the middle of the bowl because that's where it is hottest. We had to do it three times before it was 60 degrees and then we tried Mummy's and Daddy's.*

The children then wrote letters explaining their findings. This is an extract from Joanne's letter;

> *We took the temperature of Baby Bear's porridge three times and when it was just right it was sixty degrees. Then we tried the big and medium sized bowls and here are the results. Mummy Bear's porridge was 63 degrees and Daddy Bear's porridge was 65 degrees. So I think you should change 'too hot, too cold and just right' to 'too sweet, not sweet enough and just right' to make it really possible.*

Their teacher was delighted with the children's scientific research and reported that although it seemed a simple idea it had provoked a lot of discussion at the planning stage with the children keen to find out what the temperatures would be. The work had been undertaken in small groups, assisted by parent helpers and had taken a week to complete. This had enabled pupils to build up the weight of evidence. The experience encouraged the pupils to write to the publisher, telling her/him of their findings. They enjoyed the porridge too.

'Science involves a distinct way of seeing and exploring reality' (Feasey 1999). We might not always want children to consider the differences between fact and fiction but by using a favourite, well known story it is possible to stimulate scientific enquiry.

By enabling them to frame the question, ' I wonder what would happen if …' we can encourage children to make suggestions about what to do, how to do it and to see that the information they collect is a source of valuable and important evidence. As these pupils have shown, the logical conclusion is to tell other people about what they have found. In this way pupils will be engaging in science as a discipline by doing just what real scientists do.

Mathematics through story

The relationship between mathematics and narrative may, initially, seem very tenuous; one deals with logico-deductive thought whilst the other elicits the more ephemeral aesthetic of representation, symbol and metaphor. However, as with other aspects of the curriculum, stories can be a useful vehicle for the delivery of subject-specific matter and the encouragement of mathematical thinking is no exception. This point may be especially pertinent to those children who are 'reluctant mathematicians' and who lack confidence in their ability to hold numbers in their head. For such children, story can provide the alternative reality which distances them from their fear of maths. I discovered this important function of narrative one night as I was about to tell my youngest daughter her bedtime story. At school she had been struggling to remember her times tables and was becoming frustrated by them. I was concerned that she might get completely turned off and feel she was never going to grasp them.

We had a 'magic book' that my eldest daughter had loved when she was young and I decided to try it on Nanaki. The book simply consisted of my hands, held palm to palm to represent the front and back covers. The story always began with the opening of the book, hinged away from my thumbs. The character was always the same, a giant who lived in a large stone house at the top of a hill. At the beginning of the story he always awoke from his dreams, stretched and went to make breakfast. This was when the complication began because he always found that the cupboard, the fridge and the freezer were empty. So his journey began, down the hill and into the village, in search of food. It was at this point that the story changed to suit the needs of my little listener, who by now had captured the form of the giant in her imagination. As he went on his way, brushing the very tops of the trees with his elbows, carefully avoiding a passing cyclist, he accrued characteristics. As the story progressed he became the hungry, very careful giant, and so on until he had a chain of descriptive labels. On this particular occasion the shops in the village were closed. So he was a very hungry, careful, frustrated giant, who heard the baker working in the bakehouse. The giant had forgotten to bring any money so the baker agreed to give him a loaf of bread if he could tell him how many loaves he had made.

'There are six trays and six loaves on each tray. Now I'm too busy to work it all out. So if you can kindly tell me, then I'll know how many more trays I have to put in the oven,' said the baker.

'I might need a bit of help wi' that one,' replied the hungry, frustrated, baffled giant.

At this point the story was suspended as the narrator asked the little girl if they could help the giant. She readily agreed and they worked together to solve the problem. In this way 'recesses' can be built into narratives which enable the storyteller–parent–teacher to scaffold the child's thinking.

How can the problem be solved without us having to count each loaf? Which times table is it? I know what two times six is – 12, but that's only two trays and there are four more, what can we do?

Through collaborative thought existing knowledge can be reinforced and the processes of mathematical problem solving demystified, leading to a more confident and independent learner able to scan number from the higher plane of achievement. What had previously seemed abstract and insurmountable was contextualised under the subterfuge of story.

It may not always be possible for the teacher to replicate this one-to-one, caretaker role in the busy classroom but that does not negate the efficacy of story. In the tale of the hungry giant, the mathematical element was incidental, but there are published approaches that embed mathematics more firmly within mini-narratives and which position the reader as the deductive investigator. An example of this is Keeling and Whiteman's (undated) *Mathematics Through Database,* an activity pack for Key Stage 1 and 2 pupils, which uses a partial narrative to promote logical problem solving.

An example is the story of 'Digger', the account of an unfortunate incident that occurred late one night at Mrs Law's house. She awoke to discover a *huge hole* in her garden. According to her neighbour, who had been disturbed in the night by a *scraping noise*, the hole had been dug by a *large* dog. In his description of the dog, Mr Grove revealed some of its other characteristics; it had a tail which pointed towards the ground, light patches, and a collar that glinted in the moonlight. We are also told that at the bottom of the hole was a rib-shaped bone. At the end of the tale the reader is asked to identify which dog committed the dastardly crime. To help them solve the mystery pupils have a pack of twenty-four picture cards. The cards depict different dogs with varying characteristics The identity of the dog is revealed by pupils as they systematically select appropriate variables and eliminate those cards that do not apply. In order to do this they must interact with the text to check the validity of their selections, until they have one card remaining, 'Digger'.

This type of task can be easily differentiated by increasing or reducing the number of variables and by altering the readability of the text. For early readers and pupils in the first stages of learning English as an Additional Language (EAL), the story can be taped, or they can have it read to them. By making the activity a collaborative exercise involving two or three pupils, the caretaker role, which I adopted with my daughter, is shared as children scaffold one another's learning, through questions, prompts and the signalling of clues. By encouraging cooperation in learning we are attending to children's social development and are meeting the requirements of the spiritual, moral, social and cultural (SMSC) dimension in the curriculum. This activity also highlights another important feature of the primary curriculum: cross-curricular links. In this particular case, there is an obvious integration of data handling (Maths AT 4) and the location of factual material in the text (English AT 2).

History

Storytelling has long been considered a good method of teaching history. Indeed, as has been suggested elsewhere in the book, it has been a traditional means of cultural groups handing on their traditions and knowledge from one generation to another (Egan 1988:2). A good story, well told, commands interest and can lead to discussion and, therefore, the posing of historical questions. In history, as in other parts of the curriculum, the attraction of storytelling is in its narrative power, through which it appeals to children's imagination, curiosity and emotions. Storytelling can be an effective way of introducing and extending historical knowledge and vocabulary. Listening to, retelling, and creating stories are activities that appeal to children of all abilities and backgrounds. Story provides one means of both giving children access to history and, in the case of them writing their own stories based on historical events and people, of building differentiation by outcome into their work. Some children will simply adhere closely to the facts and sequence of events in their stories while others will go beyond this in an attempt to capture something of the life of the times by describing the sights, smells and behaviour of people, basing their creative thinking on primary and secondary evidence.

While the link between history and story is apparent in the very word history it is important to remember that the subject is not merely the handing on or recounting of knowledge. It is also concerned with processes. Historians undertake investigations using historical evidence; they hypothesise and they attempt to justify their interpretations by reference to available data. This balance between historical knowledge and the process of investigating that knowledge is crucial for the historian, the teacher and the learner. It is essential that history is recognised as knowing-how as well as knowing-what (Lee 1994:47). This has implications for the classroom and the way in which history is taught. While story may be a tried and trusted method of teaching history, it is important that the storyteller realises that in addition to handing on knowledge about the past they are also engaged in helping children to understand the investigative nature of history: that history is more than just telling a story.

In keeping with the notion that history is about knowing-that and knowing-how, the National Curriculum for history is based around the acquisition of particular subject knowledge (e.g. Romans, Anglo-Saxons and Vikings in Britain, the Tudor World) and the development of particular skills and understandings (understanding chronology, causation and change, historical interpretation, historical enquiry, organising and communicating). Given the importance of story to history, I want to turn now to a brief examination of the ways in which storytelling can help develop all these aspects.

Chronological understanding

There are a variety of stories that enable children to become aware gradually of the past and to place events and people within a loose historical framework. Children can follow the chronological order of events in stories and then be asked to sequence them through pictures, statements, or the retelling of the story in their own words. The National Curriculum Council's INSET resource book (NCC 1993) suggests a wide range of activities to help children develop chronological understanding through the use of story.

Change and Causation

Stories set in the past can be used as a starting point for looking at change. After listening to a story, or part of a story, carefully framed questions can be put to children to encourage them to identify changes that have occurred between the then of the story and now. They can also make comparisons within and across periods by considering the similarities and differences between the then of one story and the then of another story they have read. By listening to a variety of stories depicting different historical periods and various cultural traditions, children can be encouraged to develop their own views about the characteristic features of the periods being studied. They can be asked to consider why people in stories acted in particular ways, or the reason why an event unfolded in the way it did. Through listening to and reading stories children can begin to explore and answer questions about causation.

Interpretations of history

As we have seen, story in its various forms, including the comic format, provides one of a range of ways of representing the past and children should be encouraged to view story as another source of finding out about history. Different versions of the same historical event can be used to show how the past may be interpreted differently. Alternatively, children might be asked to rewrite part of a story to show understanding of the notion of interpretation; to demonstrate that events can be perceived in different ways depending on such factors as the age, gender, status and citizenship of the writer. For example, mass production during Victorian times impacted on people's lives in different ways. How might a woman factory worker with several children to care for write differently from the factory owner about working hours and conditions? By positioning children in the past and within different perspectives they can take on the role of writers recording events and the effects of changes from the viewpoint of an 'insider'. Of course, this is a simulated exercise and cannot be regarded as authentic, but it creates a context for understanding that documentary evidence is not absolute, that it is partial and is subject to the particularities of the life and experience of the writer. The process of history on the other hand involves the careful study and comparison of different sources of information and the gradual collection of evidence through corroboration.

By the age of seven most children should be able to differentiate between fairy stories and 'true' stories. The retelling of fairy stories and folk tales also has its place in the historical education of young children. These genres can be used to help bridge the gap between fantasy and reality (Cooper 1995) in an effort to help children appreciate that certain types of story have elements based in real life or served particular functions in societies of the past. Such is the case with many myths, which enabled people in the past to make sense of the incomprehensible, catastrophic events, or to personalise their gods and give coherence to religious beliefs. But there can be a very fine distinction between myths and stories. The great myths are vivid depictions and are likely to be influential in developing children's views of the past. There is, therefore, the obvious danger that the myth may be taken as 'real' and teachers need to make it clear to children that these stories are not based on real events and characters, though at a later stage it may be necessary to introduce the notion that some legends involve a kernel of truth. In order to couch the discussion of myths in a healthy atmosphere of caution and scepticism the teacher may need to frame leading questions such as:

- 'Did this really happen?'
- 'Why do you think this story was told?'
- 'How can we tell whether or not the story is true?'

Historical enquiry

We have already introduced the idea that stories, when compared with one another, can be used as historical sources but the same function can be achieved by using story alongside other sources. Stories can provide the means for helping children to make sense of pictures, artefacts and historic sites. In this way, a single story might help children to create a coherent view of otherwise disparate objects. Having a picture or artefact as the starting point for a storytelling session encourages children to realise that the story does have an evidence base. When children answer the teacher's questions based on the story, or ask their own questions, they are engaging in an enquiry of historical evidence, as well as the particularities of the specific story.

Organisation and communication

From an early age most children are introduced to different types of stories. When they go to school, one of the first forms of writing that will be expected of them is story. Narrative, therefore, is an integral part of the child's development and provides the child with a linguistic framework for understanding, representing and communicating aspects of their experience. Children's familiarity with story makes the narrative structure a useful model for them when organising and communicating their findings of historical investigation.

Stories and authenticity

Returning to the matter of distinctions and similarities between story and real life, teachers are often concerned that they do not have enough historical knowledge of a particular person or event in the past to make their story true. However, stories set in the past do not have to be true; they have to be authentic. While anachronism has no place in good stories about the past, imaginative reconstruction does. '... a story might be of an imagined but typical soldier in the army of Julius Caesar, but the details of his way of life, dress and weapons would be real in the sense of their being authentic.' (HMI 1986:6).

Story conveys a different type of truth to the factual account. It is not necessary for the storyteller to know every minor detail of the life of a soldier on Hadrian's Wall, but they need to know what life was like then, what the concerns and everyday routines of such men were. Being able to weave a story around the letter from home offering new socks, sandals and two pairs of underpants to a soldier 'on the Wall' (Bowman 1994:140) can be more authentic than worrying about what a particular person actually did at a particular time. Good storytellers go to considerable lengths to create authenticity. An excellent example is the story *Julius Lupus and the Raiders* (Woodhouse 1992), based on a soldier's life on the Wall. Whether or not there ever was an auxiliary of that name is immaterial, what the story provides is an authentic view of life at Housesteads Fort, based on sound historical evidence. However, we need to guard against transporting children to a totally fantastic past. By using historical evidence we want them to distinguish gradually between the imaginative reconstruction of reality and the fantasy of story. Authenticity, therefore, involves the storyteller referring to the detail of life based upon the best available evidence. In all eventuality, the bare bones of the story are likely to be true, but for the life of the narrative there must be embellishment. The juxtaposing of story with other sources of information about the past will help children to authenticate aspects of the narrative.

Storytelling and sensitive issues

Later in this chapter we look at how story can be used to deal with sensitive issues in PSHE. History too provides a wealth of opportunities and contexts for tackling sensitive issues. The past, as well as the present, is littered with the tragic consequences of the aggressiveness of the human condition. For its part, story '... allows children to swim safely in dangerous emotional or moral waters and engages them in problems and issues affecting people in the past' (Fines 1992, in Dean 1995:8). By simultaneously engaging the reader's imagination and distancing them from the harsh reality of a situation, a context can be created which enables children to empathise with characters, leading to dispassionate discussion of moral dilemmas. For some children there will be parallels in the events of the past and the events of their own direct experience. A refugee child, hearing the story of Anne Frank or the fictional character

Rose Blanche (Gallaz 1985) may well feel the story more poignantly than British born children who have not ever feared for their lives or seen their relatives executed in front of them. More generally stories set in the past can provide opportunities to raise awareness of the dangers of stereotyping or make children aware of people history forgot, such as Mary Seacole, the Black Victorian nurse who attended British troops in the Crimea (Seacole 1988). In this way stories set in the past can help promote positive images of marginalised groups.

Developing storytelling in history

To tell a story in a primary history session may seem a daunting challenge but it need not be so. There is an increasing number of published resources to guide teachers (e.g. Cox and Hughes 1990) and some publishers have been particularly active in producing stories that can be read but are probably better told (see for example the Ginn history stories for Key Stage 1 or the Ginn teachers' handbooks for Key Stage 2: Ginn Teachers' Resources 1991a, 1991b, 1992 and 1993). The essential elements of a good history story are action, drama and suspense (Farmer 1991:41) and there is plenty of material in the history curriculum to match these ingredients.

Another approach, and one that is possibly more fun, is to involve children in the development of their own stories using artefacts or pictures. Open-ended questions such as, *'who is depicted in the picture?'*, and *'Why are they there and what have they been doing?'* can give useful starting points. Stimulating children to interrogate sources of evidence and weave their imagination around visual material from or representing the past makes them aware of the importance of authenticity.

The story of Odysseus

The story of Odysseus' journey following the siege of Troy and his return to his wife Penelope is a well-known one and is available in a variety of versions. I once retold the story in digestible portions to a Year 6 class. They became hugely enthusiastic for everything Greek. The story was diarised and eventually a script was developed around Odysseus' journey, particularly his encounters with the Sirens and the Cyclops; his homecoming as a travelling vagrant who reveals his true identity to Penelope by means of his ability to draw the famed bow (a task only Odysseus can perform); and the ensuing celebration once the happy couple are reunited. However, the children were not comfortable with merely retelling the story. They were conscious of the need to get it right, to make it authentic, and began asking a variety of questions that were essential prerequisites to historical enquiry:

- When were the Greeks?
- What did the Greeks wear?
- What were their warfare and their weapons like?
- What were Greek ships like?
- What kind of celebration would they have?
- What would they eat?
- What would a Greek city look like? (An authentic backdrop was required).

The story had stimulated historical investigation with the result that children developed their chronological awareness; they began to understand the concepts of change and causation; they posed and answered questions using a variety of historical sources; and they had to organise and synthesise information into a story format that would be enjoyable. There was a balanced measure of fun and serious argument as they made props, costumes and tested food and discussed what they thought was reasonable as far as the Greeks were concerned. Almost incidentally, they gained a huge amount of knowledge about the Greeks.

Our encounter with Odysseus demonstrates why the National Curriculum states that teachers should use story as a teaching strategy at Key Stage 1 and that it is an essential tool at Key Stage 2. It showed that story has the potential to recount the past in interesting and vivid ways. It can provide a form of historical explanation and an interpretation of events in ways that engage the listener. Stories can help children develop a sense of the past and chronological awareness and provide a springboard for historical investigation. Most of all though stories should be enjoyed and enthuse children to want to go beyond this small window on the past and develop a lifelong love of history and its stories. Odysseus certainly proved to be a voyage of discovery for the children with whom I worked, and other, well-chosen stories will work for other teachers too.

Geography

The fact that stories are set in places, real places, imaginary places, hidden places and magical places invites us to use their potential to teach about local and distant regions and the people who live there. Talk to any young child about places they know, their street, where their school is, their grandma's house or where they have been on holiday, and they have the beginnings of a story about a place. Children also know about places from watching television, reading, and now through CD Rom and the internet. In recent years, the potential of story to explore places through language and pictures has been recognised (Gadsden 1991). People from the local community who have lived in other countries can also provide insights through stories of their experiences.

Through illustration and narrative, story can be used to enhance geographical knowledge and understanding as well as to promote geographical skills. Consider that great geographer *Fantastic Mr Fox* (Dahl 1998) whose cognitive map of the routes to local farms can promote literacy and cartography simultaneoulsy as children map the locality and Mr Fox's journey within it. Younger readers might be encouraged along similar lines by *Rosie's Walk* (Hutchins 1992); *The Jolly Postman* (Ahlberg and Ahlberg 1986) and *Katie Morag Delivers the Mail* (Hedderwick 1984). It is important to revisit places in stories in the context of teaching geography, as well as to extend language and literacy. Not all children have had first-hand experiences of varied landscapes and may have had limited ones of contrasting places through the curriculum. One of my overwhelming joys as a teacher is of seeing childen's amazement when they see the sea for the first time. A good story, well told or with rich illustrations, can begin the process of bringing to life a sense of place as an alternative to direct experience. Stories like *The Man Whose Mother was a Pirate* (Mahy 1987) open up new horizons. As the mother takes her son across varied landscapes to the sea we encounter a language to describe the awe and wonder of this geographic form: he '... hadn't dreamed of the BIGNESS of the sea ... He hadn't dreamed of the blueness of it. He hadn't thought it would roll like kettledrums, and swish itself on the beach. He opened his mouth and the drift and dream of it, the weave and wave of it, the fume and foam of it never left him again.' Quality stories are able to evoke the imagery of place through the power of their telling.

One of the key questions we would like children to explore is 'what is it like to live there?' Stories enable children to visit many different types of place through both everyday speech and geographic language. While the teaching of new vocabulary should not interfere with children's enjoyment, stories can provide a good springboard to teach about physical, human and environmental geography. The description and images of physical features or processes like earthquakes, volcanoes, climatic conditions and tropical islands can help children acquire an understanding of what it might be like to live in places of the world very different from their own.

Stories set in real places, particularly those told by young people, can be a powerful way to inspire discussion in the classroom about the issues faced by people who inhabit the area. Locality packs often contain stories told by children who live there. This may often be the first step to understanding some complex local, national and international issues and the impact of political decisions on the lives of people, including the children we teach. Stories can provide insight into the reasons for migration – perhaps because of war or natural disaster – and why some become homeless, stateless refugees. Organisations such as Save the Children (Wilkes 1994) and Minority Rights Group International (Warner undated) have produced high quality materials based on the stories of young refugees. Told through the authentic voice of the child, these stories provide other children, who may never encounter such real life experiences, with insights into complex issues such as civil war, sustainable development, conservation of resources and world debt.

We need to guard against using stories without considering that most were not written with the geography curriculum in mind. Some stories may contain stereotypical images of gender and ethnicity or simplistic, unbalanced images of parts of the world. It is advisable, therefore, to select stories that promote geographical characteristics while maintaining broader educational aims (Krauss 1994). However, there is an increasing range of good stories from various cultures that can be used to supplement work on distant places, and may well provide children with a more balanced overview of contrasting localities within countries. The distinctive nature of distant places is often revealed through a narrative which explores the lives of those who live there. Good examples are: *Abuela's Weave* (Castaneda 1993) and *My Grandpa and the Sea* (Orr 1990).

It can be quite difficult for both experienced and beginning teachers to encourage children to challenge stereotypes and racist views particularly if we have not addressed them ourselves. But we do need to demonstrate the distorted and often incomplete images of places and their inhabitants. The geography curriculum enables childen to have greater understanding of their lives and the place where they live, particularly when they look at the similarities and differences between their own experience and that of other children in the world. In this way we can move towards a more critical school geography (Huckle 1997) and use the opportunity that story presents to foster social justice. Carefully selected stories that promote questioning attitudes and are oriented towards geographic knowledge, understanding and skills can contribute to educating future citizens who possess a well-focused global perspective.

Environmental education

Story provides teachers with a viable means of combining several curriculum strands into a single unit of work. It is also a means by which cross-curricular themes and dimensions may be 'tethered' to the statutory components of formal education, thereby preventing them from disappearing over the edge of our 'flat earth curriculum'. There is no reason why texts cannot be used in Literacy Hour to serve several functions. Material with a historical, geographic or scientific theme, for example, may be used to examine how textual cohesion is achieved, or might be used for reading or comprehension purposes. While the primary learning objectives for the lesson must be linguistic ones, other subjects can be used as '... vehicles for literacy ...' (DfEE 1998a: 3)

Although the example that follows predates the National Literacy Framework it nevertheless demonstrates the multi functional dimension of story in the classroom. It also shows how the 'mainstream' curriculum, the non-statutory curriculum and the 'hidden' curriculum may be linked for that most pragmatic of reasons, the class assembly. Preparation for the class assembly can be time consuming and requires careful management if it is not to cut into curriculum time. It is an aspect of teaching that is rarely touched upon in initial teacher education but assembly is an aspect of a school's communal identity and an important teaching time in its own right. Many schools organise a termly or half-termly programme of assemblies on a central theme, with class teachers sharing responsibility for their delivery, on a rotational basis.

Several years ago, faced with the imminence of a class assembly on the theme of the environment, I encountered one of those moments of desperation when, with barely enough time to organise the 'event', I suffered from mental block. Several days elapsed between my realisation that a 'performance' was imminent and final inspiration. When it came, the spark of creativity was ignited by the Nine O'clock News. The sight of bailiffs scrambling through the foliage of a mature wood in pursuit of environmentalists chained sloth-like to the gnarled upper branches of a copse of majestic trees reminded me of a story I had read to my own children several years earlier.

The following day, with my class of 30 Year 5 pupils sat comfortably on the carpet, I described what I had seen. Some of them had seen it too, and most had heard about the event, which had dominated the news for several days. Through questioning we began to explore the reasons why the conflict in the trees had occurred and soon a discussion led to the problems of deforestation and global warming. Once the topic and issues were firmly framed in the children's minds, I introduced the story, '*The People Who Hugged The Trees*' (Rose 1990). Based on an Indian folktale, it is an heroic story of how a Rajasthani woman, Amrita Devi, risked her life to save the trees near her village from the axes of the maharajah. She had recognised the environmental importance of the trees which protected her village and its people from the harsh and barren desert which lay beyond. By firstly embracing the trees, thus preventing the woodcutter from doing his work, and then persuading the maharajah that the trees served a better function alive than as timber for his fortress, she secured a permanent 'stay of execution'.

As a class we considered how we might link recent events with Amrita Devi's 300 year old story. We explored the issues through improvisation; we divided the text into manageable 'chunks' and considered how we might retell the story to an audience of peers. Bit by bit, we drafted a script so that after the assembly we would have a record of our work.

Reflecting on this work caused me to realise that teaching involves the enactment of multiple actions in a single event. Not only did the story serve a pragmatic purpose (the class assembly) and enable me to combine environmental education with aspects of English AT 1 (speaking and listening), it also stimulated learning in other ways. These other 'moments of realisation' were amplified through the voices of characters in the play, and were based on talk and research in the classroom. Pupils had devised a kind of documentary prologue to the presentation which synthesised local and global issues.

Robert:	You may have seen on your TV screens the people who have built shelters in the trees to stop them being cut down.
Josef:	The Government wants to build a road to bypass the town of Newbury in Berkshire.
Vicki:	But the people who have made their homes in the trees think the trees are too important to be chopped down.
Kyle:	Farther away from home, in South America, the Amazon Rain Forest is being destroyed because the wood of the trees is sold to us in the West.
Simon:	We use the wood in buildings and furniture.

The significance of economic interdependence and the international dimension was emphasised by drawing upon scientific knowledge:

Sam:	Scientists say the loss of trees is causing our earth to become a fragile planet.
Nazia:	We need trees to make our air clean.
Peter:	Trees turn the gas carbon dioxide into oxygen which we breathe.
Charlie:	The loss of oxygen is helping to burn a hole in the earth's atmosphere.
John:	Through the hole come the harmful rays of the sun which heat up the world and cause it to get a little hotter each year.

Turning from the facts of the present with their global implications, the narrator drew attention to the past and broadened the multicultural dimension;

Hollie: Once, long ago in India, there was a young woman called Amrita. She loved the trees because they protected her village from the harsh sand storms that blew from the desert...

As well as giving the historical perspective, other messages were conveyed through the story that morning. The female protagonist was seen to triumph over the powerful maharajah by means of her persasive language. She had stood her ground, empowered by a point of principle, and was seen to lead the people of her village in non-violent action. Although these 'lessons' about gender, ethnicity and class were far less explicit than the more obvious one about the environment, they nevertheless acted subliminally, as do all messages in the 'hidden' curriculum, to help sustain the underlying values of our school. If teaching is about the enactment of multiple actions, then story is an invaluable tool in education because of its sub-textual meanings and possibilities.

Story and personal, social and health education

Through the use of story the social world of children can be brought into the classroom and made 'real'. From the relative safety of the classroom children are able to engage their imagination or draw upon actual past experience to view the social world, complete with its tensions and conflicts. This 're-creation of reality' can be empowering in that it enables children to use their critical faculties to evaluate situations, motives and relationships. While this has been a teaching strategy in educational drama there is no reason why it must be saved for the drama room or the hall, or must wait for that special timetabled slot in the week. I recall that once, following an INSET day with the organisation, Learning Through Action, I spontaneously slipped into role as a ten year old boy, Peter, during circle time. I had the pebble in my hand that we used to pass from one to the other, our little token of the right to speak. The circle of pupils sat, tense and silent, as they listened to Peter's story of conflict at home:

Peter: In my wardrobe is a little case. The other day I put some clothes in it. My mum and dad don't know yet. But I'm getting tired of it all. Everyday it's the same. My little brother is fed-up too. He doesn't say anything, but I put my arm round him and give him a cuddle at night when he cries. He doesn't really understand what's going on. He just hears the shouting from downstairs and it frightens him. I don't want to leave him, but I can't stand it either. The case is ready, and one day, very soon, I'm sure I'm going to take it out of its hiding place, creep downstairs, open the front door and go … (looking around at pupils in the circle). What do you think I should do?

Passing the pebble to my left marked the end of the exposition; the scene had been set, characters introduced and relationships sketched lightly, leaving just enough space for the fuller picture to be developed by pupils themselves. They responded sensitively to my plea for guidance and demonstrated mature perception through comment and advice.

P1:   If you do leave, where will you go?
P2:   How will you look after yourself, it might not be safe.
P3:   I think you should stay. Even if you're unhappy, at least you are at home.
P4:   I think you should go. It will be your way of telling them you've had enough.
P5:   Who will be there for your brother if you go?
P6:   I know how he feels.
P7:   Why don't you tell them how you feel. If you talk it through with them, they can see your side and stop.

The story had done what all teachers' expositions need to do, it had created a meaningful context for learning. What was happening in the classroom was made relevant and pupils were responding accordingly. The flow of talk demonstrated that they were listening to one another, instantaneously reflecting on what others had been said and extending the range of sub-textual possibilities: *where will you go … it might not be safe … tell them how you feel* …. Here are the beginnings of other stories that could provide pupils with opportunities to explore further their social world. Here too was the opportunity to hand over the story to them. So that as narrators they could be in control and exercise choice, not just about the direction the story should take, but also about the moral decisions to be made and about how emotional and psychological dilemmas might be resolved.

It was also an opportunity for pupils to feel, and to demonstrate, their empowerment. Life can throw up conflict and unhappiness in children's lives. Domestic conflict and parental separation is a real experience for an increasing number of young people but that does not mean they are powerless to act when their world is crashing about them. The advice to *talk it through with them* was an exhortation to be proactive, for children to use their voice. It was probably no coincidence that this advice followed immediately after the child who confessed to know how Peter felt. Here was another story, perhaps to be told in the privacy of the teacher–child relationship – but only if the child wanted to tell it. However, the advice might already have had an effect with the child feeling able to tell the story of *how I feel* in the right place, to the right audience at home.

In meeting the 'Standards', graduate teachers '… must … demonstrate that they … provide structured learning opportunities which advance pupils'

i.   personal and social development;
ii. communication skills;
iii. knowledge and understanding of the world …'.

(DfEE 1998b:B5b)

The use of story in the classroom, particularly when constructed around fictionalised social scenarios, provides the teacher with one useful strategy for achieving that end. Furthermore, story adds a creative injection into what may be in danger of becoming an overly prescriptive and formulaic approach to teaching.

Drama and storytelling

Drama and storytelling share many characteristics of structure and presentation and the link between the two is implicit in many of the above examples. At the heart of drama are the tensions and conflicts experienced by people in the course of living their, sometimes, quite ordinary lives. In story too, there are real or imaginary journeys with physical or moral obstacles to be overcome by the hero or protagonist. In many instances these journeys have their parallel in real life. Many of Shakespeare's plays have their origin in story, and popular television dramas are subsequently published as novels. In Education, drama has occupied an uncertain place in the curriculum since the Education Reform Act but it now appears to be making a comeback. Drama emulates the immediacy of lived experience and is, for some, an essential pedagogic tool for developing speaking and listening skills as well as insightful understanding of specific social and narrative contexts (Neelands 1992:6). It is recognised that the process of 'shaping' stories is a cognitive one, making drama a significant contributor to pupils' learning. The framework of educational drama involving making, refining, performing and responding (Arts

Council 1992) also provides a purposeful framework for shaping and exploring story. For these reasons the place of drama in relation to storytelling deserves further consideration.

For the purposes of this brief look at educational drama, I want to consider two ways in which the subject can be used to enhance understanding of story and the practice of storytelling. Firstly, drama offers both the teacher and the pupil various techniques and strategies for exploring character, relationships, thematic concerns and subtextual possibilities. Jonathan Neelands (1998: 92-8) provides a useful A-Z of conventions and techniques for structuring drama. Secondly, since the subject involves spectacle and therefore a relationship between the 'actor' and the spectator, it can be used to help pupils 'rehearse' the techniques and dramatic devices that help to bring narrative alive for both the storyteller as well as the audience.

Drama, story and the individual

If we accept that drama is about people and the resolution of conflict, then exploring stories can help us look at personal or social issues that may be extremely pertinent to the child (the outsider, bullying, not talking to strangers). The fictitious example described under PSHE of Peter wanting to leave home because of domestic conflict is a case in point. The strategy of 'hot-seating', where pupils are asked to explore characters and their motivations, can lead them to a realisation of the links between thought, feeling, action, cause and effect. While published stories provide a clear thematic focus for the teacher unused to drama (Winston and Tandy 1998: 18), drama also allows the opportunity for improvisation around invented scenarios. In this way story can be developed by pupils working through characters and their responses and relationships to one another. In such a context the teacher can help pupils develop a structure to their story by means of questioning, editing the action, relocating the drama in time and place and by making judgements about when to move the story forward. The archetypal journey lends itself to this model because it involves some kind of challenge to the *status quo*; a conflict to be resolved before order can be re-established. The context might be historical, contemporary or even fantasy. What is essential is that the drama develops from a conflict to be resolved.

Drama can be developed from simple beginnings. Take, for example, a picture of a girl holding a hamster's cage. She has tears in her eyes. Inside the cage, the hamster is dead. Many children will have pets and will have experienced the upset caused by the death of a favoured pet. They will immediately identify with the girl and her feelings. Taking this scenario, we might ask how did she get the hamster? Why was it so important to her ? How might she feel on her way to school? What will she tell her best friend when they meet in the playground? The questions invariably lead us into the unfolding of a story which might be complete in itself, or might provide the basis for further conflict. Let us suppose that as the girl is telling the story of the dead hamster she is overhead by the class bully. How might the bully use the story to exert power over the girl, knowing that her feelings are fragile? Drama postulates the 'what if' with answers becoming the very stuff of story, driving the characters, dialogue and action. If we see our lives as a series of interconnected stories, which is often how we communicate it to others, then drama and story are inseparable. With the skilful guidance of the teacher, drama can unlock the 'mysteries' of life and can help children to gain a real sense of how stories are constructed.

All stories are invariably 'slices of life'. When writers shape their stories they select from a myriad range of narrative possibilities. What is excluded resides behind, before and after the text. This subtextual residue can be fertile ground for other stories. Take for example, Jean Rhys's (1966) elaboration of the life of Mrs Rochester before she ends up raging in the attic of Charlotte Bronte's Jane Eyre, or Tom Stoppard's (1968) exploration of how Rosencrantz and Guildenstern meet their unfortunate end while searching for Shakespeare's Hamlet. In addition to these life-beyond-the-text episodes, drama offers chances for pupils to explore a narrative from alternative viewpoints; to consider how the story might sound from the voice of another character, as in '*The True Story of the Three Little Pigs*' (Scieszka 1991) in which the wolf untraditionally becomes the narrator.

Story as spectacle

The other use of drama, which involves the individual telling a story in a dramatic and engaging way, without the use of a book, is, as we saw in Chapter 3, often more daunting for both teachers and pupils alike. However, through practise, drama can help pupils gain confidence in the use of expression, gesture and voice. Familiar routines such as getting up in the morning, dressing, having breakfast and leaving for school, or shopping in a busy supermarket, can be 'told' through movement or mime. Alternatively, these quite ordinary mini stories can be presented to a small group of peers in whisper, a strong voice, a sad voice, and so on. The story can be told to create a particular atmosphere: mystery, suspense, humour. In order to emphasise the communication of meaning through expression pupils might be asked to tell viewers of the Six

O'clock News about a tragic event using a limited range of words, or the numbers from one to five. Just as the absence of one of our senses tends to make us more reliant upon and more aware of the others, so the absence of language forces us to use other modes of expression such as tone and pace of voice, facial expression and body language. Following the 'news' we can ask pupils what the newscaster was telling us and how we know. Through an analysis of how the 'newscaster' told the story, pupils can be made more aware of the specific strategies used.

By combining work on understanding texts with practise on presentational skills, teachers can help pupils develop as oral story tellers. Gaining a feeling of confidence in oneself may be more of an issue for some individuals and change will not occur overnight, but by means of a carefully structured framework within a positive and supportive environment in which pupils can explore and take risks without fear of failure, drama can assist teachers to help their pupils gain the self-confidence to find their voice.

'Cloudy' the extra-curricular cat

So far we have looked only at the place of story in the curriculum, but there is a further dimension of school to be considered. What the Cloudy stories demonstrate, and what sets them apart from our other examples, is the fact that schools develop lives of their own. No matter how the curriculum is constructed, schools are still social institutions, populated by children and adults who weave shared narratives out of the threads of their daily interactions and their relationships with one another. When the curriculum is done and dusted, what memories do we carry with us of our lives at school? When adults talk about their schoolhood they rarely, if ever, recall he pedagogic skills of their teachers, but rather the characters, the incidents (usually humorous) and the dramas that filled the spaces the curriculum could not reach.

During a recent visit to their paternal Grandmother, my daughters asked about school in her day. She began by telling them where the school was, how boys and girls were separated, how, during the Second World War, they attended only half a day because their teachers taught the evacuee children during the other half. The telling of facts was short-lived and gave way to nostalgic anecdotes. Grandmother became uplifted and animated as she told them how on her very last day at school one of her friends had dared her to ride her bike across Walton pond. Halfway across the inevitable happened, she hit a stone and the bike tipped her into the water. With a laugh she concluded how cross the teacher was as she arrived at school, late and dripping wet.

Anecdotes are the significant moments that link us to our past and personalise the social world.

'Would anyone like to hear a really disgusting Cloudy story?'

The answer was predictable. Every child wanted to hear how Cloudy, a beautiful, large (very large), smoke coloured tom cat, had left muddy paw prints in the bathroom sink. How he had proceeded to balance his way precariously around the edge of the toilet seat, lean his oversized velvet-grey body deep down into the pan and had drunk the toilet water!

For six years Cloudy was an infamous folk hero, known to every child in the school. In all six, separate classes followed his daily adventures, escapades and disasters. His recent, dramatic death, in typical Cloudy fashion (the result of eating a poisoned mouse), marked the end of an era rich in Cloudy adventures.

He is buried under his favourite apple tree where he used to hide and pounce on unsuspecting visitors. Who could forget the stifled giggles as a distinguished work colleague held forth on some deep and meaningful issue of the time while Cloudy hung upside down from the end of a low branch patting the brim of the visitor's straw hat? To everyone's intense relief, Cloudy finally crashed to the ground amid a shower of apple leaves, windfalls and hurt pride. The unsuspecting visitor was none the wiser.

Cloudy's bold and tenacious character was a constant source of delight and humour to so many children. Named by Jessica after the beautiful book *Cloudy* by Deborah King, he was the James Bond of the cat world. The son of a farm cat, he was unique from the beginning. Jessica simply could not resist the naughty, deep-grey kitten playing inside the farmer's Wellington boot while his brothers and sisters dutifully slept next to their mother. Not surprisingly, Cloudy was never a one-girl cat and Jessica had to share him with several other doting admirers, each with their own tales of his adventures. He slept in the tumble dryer, stole from the fridge, disappeared soon after tea and strolled back in the morning smelling of wood smoke. He was a real hero who captured the imaginations and interests of my pupils.

Cloudy's appeal went beyond mere admiration. He influenced children's own storytelling and story writing. The proof was the best present a teacher could ever be given at the end of the year, a book of Cloudy stories, entitled *Oh, Cloudy!* by Paula Hines, now in Year 8 but written entirely by her at the end of Year 5. They are faithful to the true events, with one or two embellishments and include the 'Oh, Cloudy!' response to all his misdemeanours. Here is one of Paula's 'Oh, Cloudy'! stories from her book.

The Airing Cupboard

One day Mrs. Smith walked into the bathroom and there were a lot of clothes on the floor. She blamed it on Emily, Frances and Jessica. This happened for a week and Mrs. Smith kept blaming it on the girls. Then, one day Mrs. Smith went into the bathroom and saw Cloudy sitting on the stool next to the airing cupboard taking some clothes out and throwing them on the floor. 'Oh, Cloudy!' said Mrs. Smith. She apologised to the girls who thought it was quite funny.

The stories and their illustrations of simple pencil drawings have been shared with, and enjoyed by, children who have taken Paula's place and who have continued the tradition of writing about Cloudy. They are not complicated stories. They do not contain detailed character sketches or a highly developed plot. They do, however, contain all the ingredients of a good short story. The key to their success is their simplicity and humour. They have been a source of inspiration for a wide variety of children, including Joe, a reluctant reader and writer. His contribution came as a complete surprise and exceeded anything he produced in Literacy Hour or extended writing sessions. Was he able to relate to Cloudy in some way?

The Christmas Tree

One time, Mrs. Smith, Frances, Jessica and Emily were decorating the Christmas tree. Mrs. Smith put the fairy on the top. Jessica put the tinsel around the tree. Frances put some of her decorations on but Emily said, 'where's Cloudy?' So Emily went looking for Cloudy but there was no sign of Cloudy. Mrs. Smith said, 'don't worry, Emily, he'll be back soon.' Cloudy came back for dinner then sat by the fire which was next to the tree. Cloudy climbed it. Mrs. Smith, Jessica, Frances and Emily went in the lounge to put some more decorations up. There was a loud 'meowwwwwwww' and Cloudy jumped out. Mrs. Smith, Jessica, Frances and Emily jumped up to the ceiling with horror. Then said, 'OH, CLOUDY!'

Alongside Carol's explanation for Joe's story is another possibility. Could it be that the Cloudy stories had become a tradition that provided him with a formula for writing; that the continual reworking of the Cloudy story framework by dozens of his peers gave him the 'scaffold' he needed in order to make that leap in confidence to independent writing?

As Carol recalls, it was only on reflection and a few years after the first telling of Cloudy stories that their impact and significance became apparent. Initially, they seemed to be just snippets and part of the daily exchange of news and events that go on in the primary classroom. However, if teachers can be part of these and get closer to their children through the sharing of real life stories, they can build trusting relationships that are likely to weather any amount of curriculum change, initiatives and frameworks. If we do not find time to share real life stories the curriculum can be empty and barren. There is a danger that we can become driven by tests and targets to the extent that we might lose sight of the fact that children have lives too. We should count ourselves fortunate when they want to share their special moments: last night's football match, the sleep-over at the weekend, the story of how Susanna broke her arm.

Cloudy was a real-life character who enriched and enlivened 'Literacy'. He brought everyone closer, helped us share experiences and make sense of them, and through him, helped us enjoy 'naughtiness' and the sense of the worth of our own stories.

For Carol's pupils then, Cloudy was a legend in his own time and beyond. Her account serves as a timely reminder that learning takes place beyond the formal curriculum and that in the hands of a teacher who is sensitive to children's interests, an aspect of the life of school can be a focus of creative thought and energy. The interest generated in Cloudy's behaviour encouraged pupils, with the support of their teacher, to create something of a literary tradition. But these stories serve another function too. They are examples of the link between a life that touches but is external to us; they are the codes that frame memory and that through memory are drawn in, become part of us – the intimate reflections of where, and who, we have been.

Conclusion

What emerges from the various contributions to this chapter is the way story can be used to enhance both teaching and learning; its versatility makes it a multi-purpose pedagogic tool. Far from being a device simply to entertain, it has the capacity to encourage and develop a range of thinking processes. It can be a vehicle for imparting knowledge as the examples in history and science have shown. These two subjects have also demonstrated its power to initiate questions and its potential to encourage children to undertake real investigation, using the authentic methodology of the subject. Through stories it is possible to frame believable contexts for discussions of moral issues. Deductive thought is made possible by means of strategies that involve sorting and classifying data using clues in an accompanying narrative. As useful as story is in the primary classroom, it must come with a pedagogic warning; the line between reality and fiction must be transparent for children, otherwise there is a danger of them confusing fictionalised narrative accounts with reality. This case has been made strongly in areas such as history. Providing that teachers are aware of the pitfalls, make their pupils equally aware, and encourage them to interrogate texts by asking questions that foster critical reflection, then story is a vital strategy for learning and the primary classroom would be impoverished without it.

References

Ahlberg, A. and Ahlberg, J. (1986) *The Jolly Postman, or Other People's Letters.* London: Heinemann.

Arts Council (1992) *Drama in Schools.* London: Arts Council of Great Britain.

Barnes, D. (1976) *From Communication to Curriculum.* Harmondsworth: Penguin Books.

Birmingham Curriculum Support Service (1993a) *Science and Technology through Nursery Rhymes.* Crediton, Devon: Southgate Publishers.

Birmingham Curriculum Support Service (1993b) *Science and Technology through Traditional Tales.* Crediton, Devon: Southgate Publishers.

Bowman, A. K. (1994) *Life and Letters on the Roman Frontier: Vindolanda and its People.* London: British Museum Press.

Castaneda, O. (1993) *Abuela's Weave.* London: Turnaround.

Christofi, C. and Davies, M. (1991) 'Science through drama', *Education in Science* January 1991, 28-9.

Cooper, H. (1995) *History in the Early Years.* London: Routledge.

Cooper, P. and McIntyre, D. (1992) 'Teachers' and Pupils' Perceptions of Effective Classroom Learning: conflicts and commonalities'. Paper presented at the Annual General Conference of the British Educational Research Association, Stirling University, Scotland, August 1992.

Cox, K. and Hughes, P. (1990) *Early Years History: an Approach Through Story.* Liverpool: LIHE.

Dahl, R. (1998) *Fantastic Mr Fox.* London: Viking.

Dean, J. (1995) *Teaching History at Key Stage 2.* Cambridge: Chris Kington Publishing.

Dearing, R. (1994) *The National Curriculum and its Assessment.* London: School Curriculum and Assessment Authority.

DfEE (1998a) *The National Literacy Strategy.* London: Department for Education and Employment.

DfEE (1998b) *Teaching: High Status, High Standards.* London: Department for Education and Employment.

Egan, K. (1988) *Teaching as Storytelling: an alternative approach to teaching and the curriculum.* London: Routledge.

Farmer, A. (1999) Storytelling in History, in Hoodless, P. (ed.) *History and English in the Primary School: Exploiting the Links.* London: Routledge.

Feasey, R. (1999) *Primary Science and Literacy Links.* Hatfield: Association for Science Education.

Gadsden, A. (1991) *Geography and History through Stories: Key Stage 1.* Sheffield: Geographical Association.

Gaine, C. and George, R. (1999) *Gender, 'Race' and Class in Schooling: a New Introduction.* London: Falmer Press.

Gallaz, C. (1985) *Rose Blanche.* London: Cape.

Ginn Teachers' Resources (1991a) *Ginn History Stories.* Aylesbury: Ginn.

Ginn Teachers' Resources (1991b) *Invaders and Settlers.* Aylesbury: Ginn.

Ginn Teachers' Resources (1992) *Invaders and Settlers.* Aylesbury: Ginn.

Ginn Teachers' Resources (1993) *Ancient Greece, Exploration and Encounters.* Aylesbury: Ginn.

Gipps, C., McCallum, B. and Brown, M. (1999) 'Primary teachers' beliefs about teaching and learning', *The Curriculum Journal* **10** (1), Spring 1999, 123-34.

Hedderwick, M. (1984) *Katie Morag Delivers the Mail.* London: Picture Lions.

HMI (1986) *History in the Primary and Secondary Years: an HMI View.* London: HMSO.

Howard, S. (1992) 'Using the performing arts as a medium for science concept development in primary school children', *Primary Science Review* **25** December 1992.

Howe, M. J. A. (1999) *A Teacher's Guide to the Psychology of Learning, 2nd edn.* Oxford: Blackwell.

Huckle, J. (1997) 'Towards a critical school geography', in Tilbury, D. and Williams, M. (eds) *Teaching and Learning Geography.* London: Routledge.

Hutchins, P. (1992) *Rosie's Walk.* London: Random Century.

Keeling and Whiteman (undated) *Mathematics Through Database.* Sutton Coldfield: K. W. Publications.

Krauss, J. (1994) '"Read all about it": using children's literature in support of primary geography', in Marsden, B. and Hughes, J. (eds) *Primary School Geography.* London: David Fulton Publishers.

Lee, P. (1994) 'Historical knowledge and the National Curriculum', in Boudillon, H. (ed.) *Teaching History,* London: Open University.

Mahy, M. (1987) *The Man whose Mother was a Pirate.* London: Puffin.

Mitra, J. (2000) in Leask, M. and Meadows, J. *Learning to Teach using ICT in the Primary School.* London: Routledge.

NCC (1993) *Teaching History at Key Stage One: NCC INSET Resources.* York: NCC.

Neelands, J. (1992) *Learning Through Imagined Experience.* London: Hodder & Stoughton.

Neelands, J. (1998) *Beginning Drama 11-14.* London: David Fulton Publishers.

Northamptonshire Science Centre (1991) *Science from Stories.* Northampton: Northamptonshire County Council.

Orr, K. (1990) *My Grandpa and the Sea.* Minneapolis: Carolrhoda Books.

QCA (1998) *Maintaining Breadth and Balance at Key Stages 1 and 2.* London: Qualifications and Curriculum Authority.

QCA (1999a) *The Review of the National Curriculum in England: The Consultation Materials.* London: QCA.

QCA (1999b) *The Review of the National Curriculum in England: The Secretary of State's Proposals.* London: QCA.

Rhys, J. (1966) *Wide Sargasso Sea.* London: André Deutsch.

Rose, D. L. (1990) *The People Who Hugged The Trees.* Scull, West Cork: Roberts Rinehart International.

Scieszka, J. (1991) *The True Story of the Three Little Pigs.* London: Puffin.

Seacole, M (1988) *The Wonderful Adventures of Mary Seacole in Many Lands.* Oxford: Oxford University Press.

Stannard, R. (1989) *The Time and Space of Uncle Albert.* London: Faber & Faber.

Stannard, R. (1991) *Black Holes and Uncle Albert.* London: Faber & Faber.

Stoppard, T. (1968) *Rosencrantz and Guildenstern are Dead.* London: Faber & Faber.

Strube, P. (1990) 'Narrative in science education', *English in Education* **24** (1), 56-60. Sheffield: The National Association for the Teaching of English.

Warner, R. (ed.) (undated) *Forging New Identities: Young Refugees and Minority Students Tell Their Stories.* London: Minority Rights Group.

Wilkes, S. (1994) *One Day we Had to Run: Refugee Children Tell their Stories in Words and Paintings*. London: Save the Children Fund.

Wilkins, V. and McLean, G. (1991) The BBC 'Science Challenge Series': *Albena and the Rock* (story from Ghana); *Five Things to Find* (story from Tunisia); *Just a Pile of Rice* (story from China); *The Snowball Rent* (story from Scotland). Crediton, Devon: Southgate Publishers.

Winston, J. and Tandy, M. (1998) *Beginning Drama 4-11*. London: David Fulton Publishers.

Woodhouse, M. (1992) *Julius Lupus and the Raiders*. London: National Trust.

Addresses

K. W. Publications, 42 Compton Drive, Streetly, Sutton Coldfield, West Midlands, B74 2DB.

Northamptonshire Science Centre, Spencer Centre, Lewis Road, Northampton, NN5 7BJ.

Southgate Publishers, Glebe House, Church Street, Crediton, Devon, EX17 2 AF.

CHAPTER 5

Narrative, school and community

In Chapter 3 we saw how children develop confidence in their ability to tell stories in the classroom when teachers acknowledge the wider world of the child. In addition to stories they may have been read or told, television, the playground, home and community provide the child with sources for individual, group and communal narratives. Chapter 4 showed how story can be an invaluable tool for curriculum delivery; how narrative can provide the context that enables the child to connect with new and unfamiliar knowledge and concepts. But we also saw how stories may be constructed from the life beyond the curriculum that children inhabit. This chapter develops further the theme of the relationship between story and the lived experience of children and their families.

Since the 1950s Britain has become an increasingly multicultural society. Inevitably, the world for many of our children includes real and fictionalised narratives that reflect the diversity brought to them by this multicultural milieu. To some extent we have already witnessed this fact through the stories which have emerged in the preceding chapters. However, in some cases, depending on the social background of the teacher, children may have a greater awareness of cultural diversity than the adults who teach them. Furthermore, children in some of our communities are incredibly adept at responding to and synthesising strands from different cultures. I recently attended the APNA Arts Festival in Nottingham, where I experienced two examples of this amazing ability. Stereo Nation, a band which included Asian and African-Caribbean musicians, and HardKaur, a young Asian woman rap artist, included in their material music, lyrics and dance that drew on at least three cultural traditions. Their young audiences were clearly in tune with, and appreciative of, this cross-cultural fusion. Young people, then, are not just part of culture, they are creators of culture; they are reconstructing forms and styles to reflect and give meaning to the multicultural reality that is their lives. We may expect that if these transformations are taking place through music, song and dance, they are also reflected in the informal storying that occurs in the home and local community.

Throughout the book we have seen that story has a valuable part to play in both language and learning development but what should be the role of story in schools that are part of this multicultural world ? All children will have a story to tell but for some it will be in a language other than English. If we consider story to be important, how can we incorporate within the curriculum tales in the other languages of Britain? Given that all children benefit from an early and continuing awareness of the richness of language, teachers working in multi-lingual communities have additional opportunities to demonstrate the breadth and depth of our multi-lingual society. In this chapter we explore the practicalities and implications of sharing stories within communities and across cultures, as part of the incredible power of narrative to bring people together for mutual empowerment and pleasure.

While there is an increasing number of picture story books depicting children from African-Caribbean backgrounds, the same cannot be said of children from other environs (Laycock 1998:86). In his report following the inquiry into the racist murder of the black teenager, Stephen Lawrence, Sir William Macpherson (1999) noted the particular importance of the education system, 'from pre-primary school upwards and onwards', as part of the wider societal responsibility to eradicate the spectre of racism from our society. The development of a broader multicultural literature, including cross-cultural storytelling, could, therefore, provide one of the means of bringing marginalised minorities into the mainstream. The stories to be told, as we shall see from Naseer's experience later in the chapter, will inevitably deal with prejudice and racism but they are also likely to include stories from the broader picture of the lives of Black and minority ethnic children, women and men. Positive as well as the negative features of our multi-ethnic society need to be authentically represented by writers who live the multi-ethnic reality of modern Britain. Within our community of diverse identities, there is a wealth of real 'life-to-text' material to be tapped and teachers are in an excellent position to bring into the public domain stories of the lives of their pupils. To do so would continue the precedent created by Chris Searle (1971) who published the poetry of his working class pupils in the East End of London. For those teachers who are not in a position to take such a radical step, the alternative is to create the demand for good multicultural stories through their position as consumers in the market place. If, as Macpherson requests and the numerous recipients of racism demand, we are to play our part in the eradication of racism from our society, a task that is long overdue, we shall need to utilise diverse and ingenious means. Story could prove to be a most powerful ally.

The teacher–narrator

In recent decades, our thinking about the role of the reader has changed dramatically. We now perceive the reader as an active participant; someone who uses their life experience to derive meaning from what is being read. The use of 'life-to-text strategies' and its counterpart, 'text-to-life strategies' (Cochran-Smith 1984, cited in Gregory 1996:81), (that is, the interplay between fiction and real life), are now considered to be essential aspects of the process of learning to read. This being the case, we might point to the dearth of readily available literature in Britain for minority ethnic children. In contrast to North America, where what might be called multicultural children's literature is flourishing, literature that depicts Britain as a multicultural society is on a very small scale. This is particularly so for readers at Key Stage 2 and presents the teacher, who may well have a number of minority ethnic pupils whom they need to develop as competent readers, with a dilemma. Should they forego what they know about the importance of providing children with reading material that reflects their own life experience by giving them a narrow diet of Anglocentric reading material? By doing so, they may well impede further the child's motivation and hence their progress in learning to read. The alternative is to write one's own material. Many teachers may shy away from writing for their pupils for a number of reasons; lack of confidence, lack of time, or lack of secure knowledge about their pupils' real life experiences, including up-to-date knowledge of their culture. The latter is a particular concern because it is easy to form stereotypical notions of culture and not so easy to remember that within each cultural or ethnic group, there is diversity. Furthermore, what may be true of a culture at one time can be old-fashioned a decade, or even several years, later.

The prospective teacher–narrator certainly needs to feel both confident and comfortable with the real life world they are about to 'fictionalise'. One way around the issue is to encourage pupils to tell stories about things that have happened to them in their lives and then rework these stories to produce authentic reading material. In this way there is a greater chance of capturing the real life perspective of the child and using it to create a 'life-to-text' narrative. One example of this approach occurred several years ago when the main High Street banks were falling over themselves to attract the young investor. As an incentive to 'teenage money', all kinds of goodies were being given away; pen-sets, hold-alls, books and so forth. One of my pupils, Naseer, realised that by moving his money around and opening multiple accounts he could acquire numerous free gifts. He confided in me that his main problem was that his money was 'tied up' in a Post Office Savings Account and that he was having difficulty completing the form to close the account. I offered to help and he brought the form to school. The completed form, together with his account book, had to be sent away in order to be processed. Several days later, when I next saw Naseer, he told me that he had done something silly. With a chuckle, he related how he had put the form in a pre-addressed envelope and posted it before realising that he had not enclosed the account book. Undeterred, he put the account book in a separate envelope and posted that too, with a little note explaining his error. 'You see Mr Gardner, the lady in the post office gave me two envelopes; one with an address on and the other one was blank.' It was at this point that realisation struck. Slowly, the grin turned to a look of sheer desperation. Naseer slapped himself on the forehead, exclaiming, 'why am I so stupid?' I looked on bemused, as he coached himself through his second big error. ' I put the book in the blank envelope and posted it.' Naseer looked up at me with something approaching terror in his eyes. 'All my money, gone. Oh, my god. Years of savings, birthday money, paper-round money. All gone!'

Initially Naseer looked unconvinced when I tried to assure him that he had not lost his money, that unaddressed envelopes would only get as far as the local sorting office, where they would be kept until claimed by the sender. He felt happier after a quick phone call. The name and address I gave, on Naseer's behalf, matched the name and address of an account book they had found in an unmarked envelope. All that was left was for the sender to verify his identity and reclaim his 'lost' goods. Naseer said he would to go straight to the sorting office that afternoon at the close of school. About a week elapsed before I next saw Naseer, walking down a corridor, looking as though the bottom had fallen out of his world.

He could barely raise his eyes as he told me that when he got to the sorting office the man there had said no trace could be found of his book. Once again, I tried to assure him that his book must be at the sorting office because I had been able to match his address correctly with the details over the phone. To resolve matters I offered to go with him after school. Later that day I gave the same details to a man at the enquiries desk who phoned through to another office and immediately confirmed the book was there. As he disappeared to get the savings book, Naseer turned to me and said, 'that man was here when I came last time. He didn't even phone, just said the book wasn't here.' Naseer paused, looked pensive and added, 'I think he doesn't like my colour'.

As Harold Rosen said in a lecture to MA students at an Open University Summer School: 'Stories about personal experience (anecdote) say something about the identity of the speaker, but they also signal the speaker's view of the way the world is.' (Nottingham University, July 1993).

Naseer's story serves as a salutary reminder that we experience our society in different ways and that that experience is influenced by our relative position in terms of factors such as ethnicity, 'race', class, gender and disability. The way we see the world is signalled in our stories but so too is the way the world sees us. Stories like this one which demonstrate the process and effect of inequality can exemplify, far greater than years of political rhetoric, the reality of the injustices experienced by some of us. Story can be a powerful persuader and a good story can be an effective agent for change.

Storytelling as social event

In many societies storytelling is an important communal event. Through narrative meanings, values and beliefs are shared across, and within, generations. As well as entertaining the imagination, narrative serves an important social function; it is a vehicle by which the older generation informs the young of its history, the means by which the social world is revealed and given coherence (Egan 1988, Bruner 1990). The links between the individual, language, identity and culture, are powerful reminders of the reasons why the languages of Britain need to be incorporated into the curriculum. Their presence in school is social affirmation of their importance and is, therefore, indicative of the value given to speakers of those languages. As Houlton (1985:14) says 'To value language and culture is to value the child'. The inclusion of a modern foreign language from Year 6 reinforces implicit messages about the languages that are excluded. French is often given prestige because it tends to be adopted by primary schools as the preferred modern foreign language. If, at the same time, the minority languages of Britain are given no place in school, what is their implied value and what value is placed on the personal and social identities of their speakers, regardless of whether they happen to be pupils in the school?

There is a tendency in British society to treat foreign languages with a sense of 'otherness', as some thing outside 'our' culture, having little relevance in the lives of learners (Meek 1996:126). While there is substantial support for promoting linguistic diversity in schools (Bullock 1975: 286; Cox 1988; SCAA 1996: 12-13; DfEE 1998: 107), evidence of its acceptance is still patchy. This is perhaps, in part, to do with the endemic monolingualism of most of British society, of which teachers are representative. Unlike the estimated 70 per cent of the world's population that uses two or more languages (Savva 1990:248), most of us in Britain, with the exception of Wales where diglossia is the norm, have a working knowledge of only one. This persistent monolingulism has tended to restrict our perspectives to the extent that we fail to recognise the linguistic adeptness of our pupils, some of whom use several languages in the course of their daily lives. This point was made apparent to me during my work as a Section 11 teacher, and later as a researcher. On occasions I was asked to give a class teacher a 'second opinion' on a pupil who had 'language problems'; did I think it was because English was an additional language (EAL), or did the pupil have learning difficulties? Of course, where EAL pupils are not verbally responsive in English, teachers experience problems assessing speaking and listening, and, given that Warnock (1978:40) estimated some 20 per cent of the school population would experience some form of special educational needs, the early assessment of EAL pupils can be critical. On many of these occasions, and after talking to the pupil, I was often in a position to tell the teacher that the pupil spoke Punjabi to older members of the family, switched between Punjabi and English with siblings, spoke Urdu at community functions, sometimes watched films in Hindi and read the Qur'an in Arabic. For some of these pupils learning French at school completed their linguistic repertoire. What was the norm for the pupil was a revelation for the teacher. At least the linguistic skills of these pupils were recognised, albeit through a third party, but it is evident that some pupils still pass through our school system without their bilingualism or, as we have seen, multilingualism, being recognised as an asset. At the end of a research interview with a Gujerati Sixth Former, he turned to me and said, 'do you know you are the first teacher who has asked me about my language'. It struck me as a great 'sin of omission' that a student could pass through nearly 13 years of formal schooling without receiving due recognition of his linguistic competence. For me, his words were testimony of the need for change in our general attitude to language. As teachers, we are in a prime position to 'influence the micro-society of the classroom by developing linguistic sensitivity' to diverse ways of communicating (Jago 1999:162-4). There is still an urgent need in Britain to reconceptualise language; to break from the notion that language invariably means *the* language – English – and encompasses a breadth of communicative codes that constitutes multilingualism.

The classroom and the language curriculum, in particular, are the sites in which to enact change. Some may argue that the primary curriculum is already overburdened and that there simply is not enough room to accommodate more; but the change required is more attitudinal than structural and involves the adoption of an inclusive perspective. In other words, we may need to modify our cultural horizons to include within the classroom the multi-lingual and multi-cultural social reality that is Britain, rather than ignore its presence. The point applies equally to schools and classrooms with few or no black and minority ethnic pupils because without this broader perspective these pupils will also be disadvantaged. They will grow up lacking the necessary 'cultural capital' to communicate effectively as young people and adults, in a society where the cross currents of different cultures coming together means that all cultures, and the social identities of those who reside in the multi-cultural social milieu, are subject to cross-cultural influence. A basic component of citizenship in such a society will be the necessary knowledge to recognise the contributions made to the nation by all our cultures. Allied to this knowledge will be an understanding of why, and how, we are the society we are.

The changes required may be small in comparison to their effect and can be incorporated into the daily life of the classroom. It is not uncommon to hear teachers calling the register in French and it would involve only a moment's explanation to extend this to other languages. So, instead of 'bonjour Sophie' … 'Bonjour, Madamoiselle', it could be, 'sat sri akal Sophie' … 'sat sri akal Miss' (Religion – Sikh; Language – Punjabi), or, 'assalam aleykum Sophie' … 'wah aleykum assalam Miss' (Religion – Muslim; Language – Urdu). My last class of Year 5 pupils enjoyed learning and using greetings in different languages. So much so that they did their own research by asking family members and friends if they knew greetings from languages we had not yet covered. Occasionally, they would catch me out by answering in a language I did not know. After teaching me and the rest of the class how to say the greeting, with its accompanying response, it too became part of our early morning repertoire and soon lost its unfamiliarity. I extended this idea in a short story I wrote for the class called 'Hi, Hello, Buongiorno'. The complete version is reproduced as a postscript to this book. In the story, three pupils play a game of greetings with their teacher. On their way to school the friends teach one another different greetings in an attempt to catch their teacher out. The first day established a convention within the narrative.

> *"Hello, girls," said Ms Cohen in a cheery voice.*
> *"Buongiorno, Ms Cohen," said Gina, Reshma and Angela together.*
> *They giggled. Ms Cohen stopped writing on the board.*
> *"Come sta?" she asked.*

> *Reshma and Angela stopped giggling. Gina looked surprised.*
> *"Bene, grazie," she replied after a pause and then said,*
> *"where did you learn Italian, Miss?"*

Each time the girls greet their teacher she replies in the appropriate language, explaining that she learned it while on holiday or from a neighbour. While the final version of the story was in the written form it nevertheless had its origins in the spoken language of our early morning interactions with one another and had emerged out of the social narrative that was the life of the class. In writing the story, one of my aims was to show that learning and sharing languages was not only normal but exciting. The girls saw it as a fun thing to do; their teacher saw it as a necessary part of living in a multilingual environment. In a simple way, the story confirmed what Rosen had said that stories reflect and reveal aspects of the writer's view of social reality. Social narrative, story and storytelling share a symbiotic relationship; the one drawing upon the other for sustenance before feeding back through its communicative power to reflect and sharpen awareness.

There is a need in a multi-cultural and multi-lingual society for more and more stories to reveal this reality. While some publishers have responded to this by producing bilingual and multi-cultural stories, these are mostly aimed at the early years and Key Stage 1. Sadly, there is a dearth of such material for children in the middle years of their schooling. Given that literature is both a socially produced phenomenon and a signifier of cultural preoccupations, the implicit message conveyed by our society is that the languages and cultures of young minority ethnic children are to be accepted. However, the absence of suitable resources in later childhood and adolescence implies that the same children are expected to 'grow out of', or at least, 'leave behind', their language and culture as they mature. This is a case of multiculturalism giving way to assimilationism as the child proceeds through the education system. Since there is no official government policy underpinning this process and since publishing houses are commercial enterprises that respond to the market place, we can assume the diminution, if not exclusion, of minority ethnic languages and cultures in children's literature is an example of unwitting institutionalised racism. This is a social phenomenon then, that needs redressing by action within social institutions, including commercial enterprises. Good intentions by individual teachers acting in isolation may have a positive effect on their pupils, but these are like ripples in a tiny pond as opposed to waves in an ocean.

Children as storytellers

While teachers can develop the expertise of storytelling, children too can become skilled in the art. Indeed, it is a requirement of the English Programmes of study at Key Stage 1 and Key Stage 2 that we provide pupils with opportunities to tell 'real and imagined' stories. The next example, taken from my work as a Year 5 Team Leader, while working at Bushfield Middle School in Milton Keynes, shows how, with guidance from their teachers, pupils can be adept storytellers and that storytelling can be a useful means of bringing children together.

The project I am about to describe makes apparent that the act of oral storytelling has both psychological and social power, as well as being a literary event. As the narrative unfolds the intimacy between the story teller and the audience grows. Through the rhetorical devices of voice, expression and gesture, words are animated, capturing imaginations temporarily drawn into an alternative reality that is telescoped in time. The effect on the listener is cathartic. I recall how, as a child, I often felt refreshed by listening to a good story well told, as though emerging from a relaxing sleep. It would not be surprising to find that the emotional and psychological effects on the listener are significantly similar to the effects of hypnosis on the individual undergoing therapy. As human beings then, we possess an extraordinary capacity to close down our senses to the immediate external world and immerse ourselves in the fictitious reality of narrative. Regard the faces of children listening to a good story; they appear transfixed with their eyes wide open and mouths agape, imagination and emotions engaged. Stories simply 'do things to people' (Protherough 1983:3). Summarising the work of several research projects that studied children's responses to stories, Protherough identified six 'things' that stories did to them; 1) they caused physical changes (feelings of dizzines, or nausea); 2) they prompted the recall of past experiences; 3) they caused readers to speculate on ' what might be'; 4) they instigated changes in attitude; 5) they encouraged empathy with characters; 6) they brought about emotional change. Story reading and storytelling can be a truly seductive experience and we might add to Protherough's list the potential of story as a medium for teaching and learning.

Given the power of the event then, the act of storytelling can be an extremely effective strategy for establishing and building relationships between children of different ages. Book making was our Design Technology theme for the Summer Term and storywriting our focus in English. At our medium-term planning meeting the year team had decided to integrate the two subjects which was an obvious thing to do, but we wanted to give pupils a real purpose for writing stories and for making them into books. We needed to provide them with real readers who would become an authentic audience. In doing so, we intended to extend the range of people for whom our pupils had written (KS2: AT3 1b). Within our design theme, one of our learning objectives involved making simple mechanisms to produce movement (DFE 1995, KS2: PoS 5c) and we identified children's pop-up books as a resource for investigation. Allied to this enquiry work was a research phase in English involving a study of the characteristics of narrative and its presentation for younger readers (KS2: AT3 1c). After consulting with colleagues at one of our feeder schools which was a few hundred yards down the road, each class wrote a letter to children in each of the Year 3 classes at Wyvern. Year 3 was chosen because these were the children who were due to transfer to Bushfield in September. The letter informed the younger children of the book project and invited them to provide information about story books they had read and had liked. This 'impromptu' market research provided us with titles, authors and themes favoured by the younger pupils. During the first half of the term, copies of the identified stories and authors were bought, borrowed and read, leading to class discussions about the different storylines; the use of illustrations; the way characters were introduced and developed; the kind of themes covered and writers' use of language. In parallel to this work, our pupils drafted their own stories and experimented with design. The opening extract from Emma's story demonstrates how these literary investigations and subsequent imitative drafts of existing stories helped pupils to 'fine tune' an authentic narrative voice. The origin of her story, entitled 'Giraffe's Troublesome Day', is clear from the occupation of its protagonist and his companion.

> Early one morning, just as the day was dawning, Postman Giraffe and Jess, his black and white cat, were sitting in their bright blue van driving to the village to pick up the post to deliver. As they drove towards the village, Giraffe started hearing strange noises coming from underneath the bonnet. Splutter, cough.

As well as introducing the main character Emma's exposition suggests the story setting and foreshadows a vital ingredient of story: a problem to be encountered and overcome. Her language is literary, evocative and draws upon aural 'images' in the form of onomatopoeia. Imitation of an existing tale has provided a useful 'scaffold' for Emma's own venture into story.

When the books were finished, the authors took their stories to Wyvern and read them to the Year 3 Pupils. As I moved quietly around the hall listening to clusters of authors and readers, the significance of storytelling as a compelling social event became apparent. There were requests to 'read it again' which signified not only the enjoyment of the listeners but the accomplishments of the writer/storytellers also. Significantly, the collaboration between narrator and audience established relationships that lasted beyond the moment. It had helped create for the younger children an image of the older pupils that they would bring with them when they transferred to middle school. These bigger, older people were no longer unfamiliar figures, a potential source of anxiety for the younger ones. Instead, they were expressive, creative people, able to share and entertain and they stood for models of what the younger children could achieve in their new school. On arrival at the school, the newcomers had a reason to re-engage their more senior counterparts: 'Hi yer, you came and told us that story.'

The ice had been broken. But perhaps more than this had happened. It is possible that we had begun to rediscover the value of storytelling as a form of bonding; a means of bringing together people who might otherwise never have engaged one another in purposeful social interaction. It is interesting to note that at the beginning of the twenty-first century (according to the Christian calendar), at a time when televisual texts are becoming more readily available through the use of CD Rom and the internet, at a time of increasing political concern about the fragmentation of family life and community networks, that most ancient form of human intercourse, storytelling, retains its indelible power to bring people together. Our final example also demonstrates the empowering quality of story.

Stories to build bridges

When children go to school for the first time or transfer between schools it can be a stressful and sometimes traumatic experience for them. If children are worried and unhappy about starting school parents are rightly anxious about the future. The transition from home to school or from one school to another can require careful management. Most schools handle matters with sensitivity by meeting with parents beforehand and by involving children in pre-entry visits to meet their teacher and to familiarise themselves with their new environment. The following example illustrates further how the involvement of children in writing their own stories can play a supportive function at this point of transition.

Teachers at Shepherdswell First School in Milton Keynes initiated a novel way of combining home–school visits and language development with the process of entry to school for preschool children. When making a home visit, the child's prospective teacher took photographs of the family in their home. These photographs were combined with others, given by the family, to produce the child's first book at school. The child, the teacher and members of the family worked on a text to accompany the photographs. Although the text did not always adhere to a conventional narrative, it was, nevertheless, illustrative of significant people, favourite pets, special places and important moments in the child's own life story. In cases where the family was literate in more than one language, parents were involved in producing a dual-language book. When children arrived at school what they saw were images of themselves and their family, proudly displayed. The school had taken account of the social and emotional well-being of its future pupils and it had begun to empower pupils and parents by demystifying school as a separate social institution, remote from family and home. The incorporation of the home languages and cultures of bilingual pupils was an important factor in this process of inclusion and empowerment (Jago 1999:161). However, as stated above, incorporation of language and culture must extend to the child's whole school career and not be restricted to the early years; otherwise there is likely to be dislocation of school from home. In this event, the effects on self-esteem and positive self-identity, sustained by the work of dedicated teachers in the early years, are likely to atrophy.

In the act of producing the book the school had accomplished a tremendous feat; the threshold between home and school had been crossed, not just by the child but by the whole family. Although this type of home–school liaison is initially very time consuming, an analysis of the strategy reveals it to be a multifunctional one, with benefits for all involved. Based as it is on a collaborative activity between home and school, it provides a real purpose for parents and the teacher, and the teacher and the child, to get to know one another before the child actually starts school. It is also likely that the teacher will know and understand more about the child's background, family structure, experience and interests, than they would by reading the school's admission form, or by means of direct questions. In the case of minority ethnic children, the teacher can learn much about the child's religion and home languages and, more importantly, the school is demonstrating from the outset that the languages and culture of home are being valued. This is likely to give both the parents and the child greater confidence in the school. The presence in the classroom of dual-language texts also signals to English monolingual pupils that the school values linguistic diversity. This is an important lesson to be learned at an early age because it can change significantly the attitudes of monolingual pupils both to learning a second language themselves and to hearing languages other than English spoken around school. This latter point is no inconsequential matter. Studies have shown that monolingual pupils who lack a positive attitude to linguistic diversity sometimes use ridicule and harassment, to 'police' the language of their bilingual peers to the extent that the latter are pressurised into renouncing all knowledge of their home language (Savva op. Cit.). The Shepherdswell's 'project' had other important lessons to do with writers, texts and reading. The construction of the text took place on the child's 'home territory' and involved collaboration. The location of the text, within the child's own experience, and the nature of its making can help to demystify for the reader the essence of books and their writers. To demonstrate that the contents of texts evolve from one's own personal experience and develop in a social context is a valuable lesson about the production of literacy. The books, based on experiences and characters from the child's own life story, became the first reading material at school.

What may have begun as a strategy to initiate home–school liaison and to ease the child over the traumas of starting school proved to be an effective way of encouraging young children's engagement with text. By incorporating home languages, the linguistic and cultural diversity of the local community was brought into the classroom in a very positive way. In the stories of these young lives were the visual and written images of their individual and social identities; each one of value, each one to be shared.

Conclusion

In this chapter we have seen schools as focal points in the community and teachers who have acted as mentors, tapping the creative capacity of pupils and encouraging them to become real makers of social cohesion in their communities. Without recourse to glossy prospectuses, poll position in league tables or glowing OFSTED reports, schools such as Shepherdswell and Bushfield were, even if unwittingly, communicating something of their ethos and educational values to their immediate outside world. At the heart of these projects, involving story writing and storytelling, were educational objectives. Their outcomes included not only the learning of the pupils involved but their parents too. In the case of Shepherdswell, this was through the direct involvement of parents; in the case of Bushfield it was by means of the supplementary stories, or anecdotes; pupils invariably told their parents about their experience when they got home. By turning their creative energy from the inside outwards, these schools were able to use an educational project involving story to build links with parents, community and future pupils. With an economy of means, these creative enterprises served educational, emotional and social purposes simultaneously.

References

Bruner, J. (1990) *Acts of Meaning*. London: Harvard University Press.

Bullock, Sir Alan (1975) *A Language for Life: Report of the Committee of Inquiry* [in *Reading and the Use of English*] *appointed for the Secretary of State for Education and Science under the Chairmanship of Sir Alan Bullock*. London: HMSO.

Cochran-Smith, M. (1984) *The Making of a Reader*. Norwood, New Jersey: Ablex Publishing.

Cox, B. (1988) *English for Ages 5-11: Report of the English Working Group*. London: HMSO.

DFE (1995) *Design Technology in the National Curriculum*. London: HMSO.

DfEE (1998) *The National Literacy Strategy*. London DfEE.

Egan, K. (1988) *Teaching as Storytelling: an Alternative Approach to Teaching and the Curriculum*. London: Routledge.

Gregory, E. (1996) *Making Sense of a New World: Learning to Read in a Second Language*. London: Paul Chapman Publishing.

Houlton, D. (1985) *All Our Languages: a Handbook for the Multilingual Classroom*. London: Edward Arnold.

Jago, M. (1999) 'Bilingual children in a monolingual society', in Davis, T. (ed.) *Young Children Learning*. London: Paul Chapman Publishing.

Laycock, L. (1998) 'A way into a new language and culture', in Evans, J. (ed.) *What's in The Picture?* London: Paul Chapman Publishing.

MacPherson, Sir W. (1999) *The Stephen Lawrence Inquiry: Report of an Inquiry by Sir William Macpherson of Cluny*. London: HMSO.

Meek, M. (1996) *Developing Pedagogy in Multilingual Classrooms: the Writings of Josie Levine*. Stoke on Trent: Trentham Books.

Protherough, R. (1983) *Developing Response to Fiction*. Milton Keynes: Open University Press.

Savva, H. (1990) 'The rights of bilingual children', in Carter, R. (ed.) *Knowledge about Language and the Curriculum*. London: Hodder & Stoughton.

SCAA (1996) *Teaching English as an Additional Language: a Framework for Policy*. London: SCAA Publications.

Searle, C. (ed.) (1971) *Stepney Words*. London: Reality Press.

Warnock, H. M. (1978) *Special Educational Needs: Report of the Committee of Enquiry into the Education of Handicapped Children and Young People*. London: HMSO.

CHAPTER 6

Language, story and identity

The National Literacy Strategy, with its emphasis on the study of language at word, sentence and text level, implies a model of language which is self-contained; a specimen to be inspected in the laboratory. However, to view language as though it were an object, devoid of the social context of its creation and use, is to dislocate it from the field of human interaction within which language derives the full quality of its meanings. An analogy might be the difference between the study of a fish in and out of water. With the life drained from it, we can take our time to inspect the fish and its various parts. We can see the construction of its fins and gills; feel the texture of its skin and see how its scales overlap like tiny silver shields. While this may be valuable, can we really claim that at the end of our study we know what a fish is? Is it possible to get at the essence of the fish, bereft as it is of life? In water, however, we get a different perspective of the fish. It appeals to different senses. By means of its mobility; its slow grace, its speed and swift change of direction, the way it catches the light and throws it back to us, the fish has the power to both calm and excite. Just as we need more than one way of studying the fish, so we need different ways of looking at language. Language then, is a dynamic being; one that refuses to keep still and is constantly slipping in and out of our grasp. It is often through the liveliness of storytelling that children first come to appreciate the full dramatic texture of language in use.

In this chapter, we explore further this difference between language as object and language in use by drawing upon the perspectives and experiences of bilingual children and adults, as well as the teachers and adults who work with them. We shall see how being a member of a minority group would seem to sharpen a sense of self and one's relationship to family and community. Language is seen as the binding thread pulling together the individual and their community. We develop the theme of linguistic diversity in the classroom, begun elsewhere in this book, by focusing more specifically on the place of dual-language story and describe a project undertaken by two of our colleagues, Lorraine and Nick Hubbard (Hubbard and Hubbard 1989) as they worked with young bilingual learners on the story of Topiwalo, the Hatmaker. A comprehensive language curriculum is one which combines the study of how language is constructed with children's implicit knowledge of how language operates, and how it has meaning for them beyond mere words.

Language as object and language in use

As suggested above, language can be described and analysed on several levels. At its most basic it is a set of sounds (phonemes) with accompanying visual marks (graphemes) which are arranged in socially agreed forms to create units of meaning (morphemes). At another level, these basic units combine to form individual words (lexis) which name and describe the material and abstract entities of the physical, human and metaphysical world. The binding element of a language, and the component that gives it coherence, is grammar (syntax). Through the practised manipulation of these elements, based on sound knowledge of the conventions of a language, speakers are able to create and re-create an infinite variety of meanings (semantics). It is this ability to be creative with language that is the hallmark of 'communicative competence' (Hymes 1974). However, if our description of language stopped here we would only be telling half the story of its immense communicative power. Language is acquired and used in social contexts, and meanings are derived as much from language in use, as they are from its lexico-grammatical structure. From the field of sociolinguistics we have learned much about how and why speakers vary their language use in different social situations. Such factors as the subject matter and institutional setting, the nature of relationships between speakers and the mode of communication all influence the language we use (Halliday 1978). Through language we not only convey our thoughts and feelings but signal our social identity. The way we speak, our choice of words and the manner with which we organise them convey where we come from, both geographically and in terms of our social class background (Trudgill 1983). This recognition of the importance of the social dimension of language was reflected in the Key Stage 1 Programme of Study for English:

> Pupils should be encouraged to develop confidence in their ability to adapt what they say to listeners and to the circumstances, beginning to recognise how language differs, *e.g. the vocabulary of standard*

English and that of dialects, how their choice of language varies in different situations.
(DFE 1995:5).

The social implications of language use and the importance of language as an indicator of social identity have become even more significant in our increasingly multilingual society. For some readers, familiar with life in a multi-ethnic community where Punjabi, Patois, Urdu, Gujarati or Sylheti, might juxtapose easily with the traditional lingua franca which may seem an obvious point, but for others, who have had little or no contact with Britain's rich linguistic diversity, it may come as a surprise to learn that approximately 200 languages are now spoken in Britain and that speakers of other languages now make up 7 per cent of the school population (SCAA 1996). Speakers of minority languages are acutely aware of how the relationship of self, family, community and social identity are embedded in their language. By means of a small scale ethnographic study of attitudes to language use amongst Sikh Punjabi speakers, I explored this issue. When asked why their first language was important to them, the following responses were typical:

'... because it is my mother tongue ... it is my identity ...' (Talgeet, aged 54)

'... because our culture is based on it ...' (Harpinder, aged 35)

'It provides an important link with the Indian community. If I couldn't speak Punjabi I would be excluded, culturally.' (Mandeep, aged 24)

' ...it is the only language I can communicate to my family with. Although English could be used it doesn't come naturally when speaking to my family. Punjabi was established early on and it is our natural language.' (Ravinder, aged 20)

'It is my family language. Therefore, if I spoke English [at home[I would feel different and not fit. It has to do with a feeling of belonging.' (Manjeet, aged 13).

The similarity of their responses, given during individual face to face interviews, signifies the extent to which language is a powerful mark, not only of individual and group identity, but of communal solidarity also. The point was made equally forcefully in the 'Cox Report' (DES 1989):

> Because language is a fundamental part of being human, it is an important aspect of a person's sense of self; because it is a fundamental feature of any community it is an important aspect of a person's sense of social identity.
>
> (para 6:18, quoted in Carter 1990)

Identity is one factor, but there are clearly other dimensions too, including the affective function of language. As Ravinder implies, the language one learns as a child creates and sustains emotional bonds between family members, to the extent that certain subjects can only be discussed through the medium of one's first language. For example, the discussion of family issues through the medium of English would not necessarily carry the same emotional and cultural resonance, with the result that both intended meanings and the relationship of speakers may be impaired. We might add to this the existential function of language, because it is through and with language, in socially meaningful contexts, that we learn about our world; it is the means by which we cement our relationship to the world and all who inhabit it. Language provides us with the symbolic code with which to conceptualise the world and to refine continually our mental representations of it. Language and thought go together, but we learn to think as we learn to speak; through social interaction, which is itself influenced by culturally specific practices as Shirley Brice Heath (1988) admirably demonstrates in her cross-cultural and cross-class study of a small community in the Southern States of the USA. The dual planes of learning, that is, learning by means of language as a form of culturally embedded social interaction, followed by the pyschological plane, or internalisation of experience through language, was made explicit in the work of Vygotsky (1986). A child's first language is, therefore, a crucial point of emotional, psychological and cognitive anchorage.

For this reason, it is important to understand the fullness of the child's social and linguistic development and ensure that we do not create a proscriptive environment in which the child feels their home language and culture must be left at the threshold to school (Bullock 1975). Bilingual stories and story telling in the classroom provide one means by which teachers can affirm the individual and social existence of their pupils who come from minority ethnic backgrounds (Gravelle 1998).

Bilingualism in education

The concept of educating the 'whole child' has long been a hallmark of British primary education. Given the fact that our society is an increasingly multilingual one, the inclusion in school of the 'other languages of Britain' is an essential prerequisite if we are to uphold tradition while simultaneously meeting the needs of our bilingual pupils. While dual-language storytelling in the classroom is the obvious medium for both affirming social identity and extending knowledge of language, for many teachers there has been a degree of ambivalence attached to the use of more than one language in school. This may be attributed to the way research of bilingualism has reported conflicting findings. Although early studies of bilingualism concluded that learning two languages required academic acumen and that it was not a worthwhile pursuit for the 'less able', the 1970s brought about a change in attitudes as the result of the publication of more enlightened reports (Gregory 1996:6). Research now suggests that learning two or more languages has at least three cognitive advantages (Jago 1999:157-8). Firstly, it can lead to a broader view of social reality because of a speaker's access to more than one language and culture. Secondly, it enables a speaker to gain clearer insights into how language works; to see language as a carefully structured symbolic system. Within the confines of monolingualism, there is a tendency to view the essence of an object and its name as integral; a table is a table, but to a bilingual child the object is separate from its name, which is simply an arbitrary tag for the 'thing'. Thirdly, it improves a speaker's ability to apply ideas across contexts, leading to a more efficient capacity to solve problems. That is not to say that monolingual pupils do not possess these capacities, but that bilingual pupils may possess them, on average, to a greater extent than their monolingual counterparts. Biliteracy brings further advantages because it familiarises the reader with a wider range of literacy styles and literacy practices (NATE 1998). Research has also suggested that languages differ in terms of surface features only and that, at a deeper level, there is much similarity between them. This would lead to the conclusion held by Cummins (1984) that proficiency in one language enhances and speeds up the process of acquisition in a second. These findings have important implications for the education of Britain's bilingual pupils and need to be reflected in the practice of those seeking Qualified Teacher Status.

With the exception of Wales, where the National Curriculum can be taught in Welsh, Britain has never adopted a formal approach to bilingual education, unlike some of its European and North American counterparts. However, through Section 11 funding (now the Ethnic Minority Achievement Grant) bilingual teachers and classroom assistants have enabled a more multilingual perspective to pervade schools and classrooms, especially in those areas where teachers, head teachers and governors have been receptive to linguistic diversity and have been aware of research findings similar to those referred to above. One of the ways in which Britain's minority languages have been recognised in the classroom is through the telling of bilingual stories. Initially, these tended to be based on traditional tales from the Indian subcontinent which were carefully recorded and reproduced by staff working at local multi-cultural resource centres. Gradually, the need for good quality dual language stories encouraged some publishers to realise the educational demand. Following a fertile decade, from around 1985, during which their publication was quite prolific, we have returned to fallow times with very little new material in the field. In a survey of publishers, conducted for the purposes of this book, the reduction in demand for the languages of the Indian subcontinent was noted, with some publishers indicating an increase in demand for European languages. Today then, the production of dual-language stories is still confined to a small group of dedicated publishers, such as Mantra and Magi.

One possible explanation for the fall in demand for dual-language stories in, say, Punjabi and English or Gujarati and English, is that as minority ethnic families become more settled and English becomes more important as the language of daily life, the first language is displaced until there ceases to be a need for literacy in it. However, such a suggestion does not take account of the wider experiences, certainly of our British Asian communities. Returning to Harpinder, referred to above in my sample of Punjabi speakers, she added an enlightening comment during the interview:

> People felt that Punjabi was going to die out, particularly people of our age (30s to 40s) who had forgotten some of their language. They didn't want their children to miss out. When people came here to survive many people felt that had to become modern i.e. adopt British habits of food, clothes etc. They did this and then learned they were not being accepted, they made a sacrifice for nothing and then came back to their culture because it is more fulfilling.

Faced with unwelcoming and sometimes hostile social environments, there may be a tendency for some second and third generation minority ethnic groups to return to their language and culture where they can regain security and solace. Earlier we discussed the importance of language and culture and one's sense of identity within them. Harpinder's comments suggest the enduring nature and long-term survival of minority ethnic cultures and languages in Britain which reaffirms the need to give positive expression to them in British classrooms. How can this be achieved when the vast majority of teachers do not speak the languages of their minority ethnic pupils? Furthermore, given that the curriculum has become more prescriptive and centralised since the Education Reform Act leading to the intensification of teachers' work (Apple 1986, in Woods 1995:3), what opportunities are there for teachers to plan for linguistic diversity?

Below, we look at the work of two monolingual colleagues who undertook a small project with a group of mainly Punjabi-English bilingual pupils in which a dual-language Indian story was used. Their work suggests that monolingual teachers can facilitate the use of the child's bilingualism, and that no matter how prescriptive the curriculum may appear, there are still spaces to be found within which specific cultural knowledge may be explored while simultaneously meeting the demands of statutory orders.

Topiwalo, the hatmaker

Working with a group of five six-year-old children for whom English was an additional language (EAL), Lorraine and Nick Hubbard sought to explore how monolingual teachers, like themselves, might develop cultural and linguistic diversity as an important element of the classroom (Hubbard and Hubbard 1989; see also Grugeon *et al.* 1998:29). The school had a substantial majority of Asian pupils and the group with whom they worked was representative of the local community. The work took place over five forty-five-minute sessions, preceded by an introductory session of half an hour. As a result of their findings Lorraine and Nick Hubbard suggest that monolingual teachers, even when they have a limited knowledge of their bilingual pupils' cultures and languages, can, nevertheless, find ways of engaging them in such a way that diversity is supported while simultaneously meeting the needs of the mainstream curriculum. The following description is taken largely from their own written account of their work with the children.

The Practical Sessions

Session One
The session began with a reading of the story to the children in English, but attention was drawn to the Punjabi in the book. The Punjabi audiotape accompanying the book was played to the children who then tried to follow the Punjabi script. The children were keen to compare the two scripts and tried to match them word for word. Fortunately, one of us knew a little about the structure of Punjabi and was able to tell the children that it was not necessarily appropriate to match the words directly as the verb in Punjabi, unlike English, is generally placed at the end of the sentence. Also the lack of an indefinite or definite article alters the structure of the language as written. A further difference is the use of a line instead of a full stop to demarcate sentences. Despite our relative lack of knowledge of the children's first language, we believe they learned a great deal about language through these initial discussions of the text. What became apparent to us from an early stage of our work with

111

the group was the ease with which these children moved between their languages. Code switching was a particular linguistic skill, no doubt acquired through the daily use of more than one language. The discussion also encouraged us to talk about other languages we could speak.

Session Two
After recapping the previous discussion, the session involved the children painting pictures of the story as a prelude to them writing it in English. This enabled them to reflect on the book and to re-enter it imaginatively in order to retell the story in their own words. The re-created stories and painted illustration were shared by the children in an assembly at the end of the week.

Session Three
The playing of the audiotape in Punjabi prompted the children to want to make their own. Before they began to record we suggested the finished tape could be sent to the deputy head teacher, a Punjabi speaker who was away ill at the time. The children liked the idea, deciding the tape might make him feel better. It also provided the children with an authentic audience and a real purpose for telling the story in their first language. They were unable to read the Punjabi script but opted instead to tell the story using the pictures in the book for guidance. At this point it was necessary to create a positive role for the one child, Sirisha, who spoke English only. When the question of what to do was raised, it was Sirisha herself who proposed a solution; she would record the story in English in her own words for the benefit of those children and adults who could not understand Punjabi. The English version would introduce the children's own version of the story. With no more than a cursory discussion about the story with her, she recorded her version in English, adding humour, her own comments and descriptions of situations. Another child, Rakesh, suggested Sirisha could learn the end of the story in Punjabi and say it with them into their tape. While Sirisha seemed satisfied with the suggestion, we felt something else was needed if she was to be more fully integrated into the Punjabi version. Other storytelling tapes with which we were familiar began with a musical introduction and we suggested their tape could begin in a similar way. Sirisha was delighted and decided to use a tambourine. This was the signal for others in the group to join in. The children sought out the school's tabla (Indian drum) and soon what had been intended as a minor feature began to sound like a discordant musical experiment as all five launched into an accompaniment, noted more for its enthusiasm than its musical quality. Clearly, the period of experimentation was necessary in order to create a sound that was both

rhythmic and pleasant to listen to. Finally, it was the tabla which led and gave focus to the music. In fact, this proved to be the most popular part of the tape.

Session Four
This session provided an opportunity for the children to tell the story in Punjabi. We sat down in a group and Rakesh, as the most confident, began to tell the story. But he eventually faltered and the others were slow to pick up the thread. As a result, we referred to the book and used the pictures to help the children to recall the story. They practised in turn using the pictures and quickly prepared themselves for the recording. On reflection, this process of the children retelling the story in their first language was an obvious point at which our monolingualism was a disadvantage. We could not tell how well the children were relating the story. Was it accurate? If we had known Punjabi could we have prompted them more to explore the richness of oral story telling? On the other hand, perhaps we overestimate the teacher's role in the process. What was evident was the children's delight and amusement when they heard their voices, causing them to comment to one another in both Punjabi and in English.

Session Five
Working from an idea that Lorraine was given by a student, we suggested to the children that we make a play out of the story by using puppets. This session was given over to making them. In order to achieve a quick result we used pea sticks and paper plates. A decision had to be made about which characters to portray and this involved us returning to the book to identify the characters who were essential to the story. It was decided that Topiwalo and five monkeys were needed. Up to this point, we had played a leading role as facilitators in the discussions, but as the pupils made their puppets we receded into the background. Our passive role in this session possibly allowed the pupils greater freedom to switch between Punjabi and English. Occasionally we would interject, asking for the Punjabi equivalent of words relevant to the story.

'What is hat?'
'Topi.'
'What's the Punjabi for monkey?'
'Bandra.'
'How would you say cheeky monkey in Punjabi?'

With delight the children answered each question and gained a sense of achievement at having something unique to teach their teachers. They taught Lorraine the different words their mothers used to tell them off, as well as the words a teacher would use.

113

It was during this session that another development occurred. There were a number of artefacts in the area where we were working. Sukhbir showed Lorraine a Sikh knife, taught her the correct Punjabi word for it (kirpan) and explained its importance to Sikhs. Our work with the children seemed to be empowering them. As they grew in confidence, so they began to share a knowledge and understanding of their own culture. Alongside this development, the children decided they wanted to present the play to the others in their class. For this more puppets were needed, for example, for the children in the book. There was also the tree to make and Topiwalo's cart. A production was obviously going to involve more work than we initially had intended.

Session Six
With the production in mind the children began to rehearse. Instead of referring to the book, they worked from memory and used their imaginations. They had little experience of preparing to show their work and Lorraine had to remind them that people would be watching their play and that there were practical considerations such as facing the puppets towards the audience. Unfortunately, the end of term drew near and the children did not complete their production. However, as those involved in educational drama would attest, it is not the end product but the process that is all important (Way 1967; Shuman 1978). So what educationally had actually happened during this work and what had been achieved?

Teaching and learning in the Topiwalo Project

As teachers, Nick and Lorraine had learned a great deal not only from the children themselves but also about the process of working with children for whom English is an additional language. They emphasise that the children's knowledge of two languages and cultures provided them with a major resource as they used their imagination and knowledge to further their own awareness, as well as that of their teachers. For example, it was discovered that as bilingual children switch between languages in their repertoire they show an increasing understanding of the role language plays in the expression of their ideas and emotions in different circumstances. If teachers can provide opportunities for pupils to code switch it is likely that they will extend their social and academic understanding. The problem of monolingualism on the part of the teacher is not an insurmountable one, as Nick and Lorraine demonstrate. They also suggest that what emerges from the example of their work with bilingual children is that the relationship between teacher and pupil is transformative, in the sense that each party is developed and changed by the other. It would seem the teacher's receptiveness to learn from her pupils and her willingness to provide guidance and the scope for them to play with language are the key issues.

The interactive and collaborative nature of the teacher–pupil relationship clearly had benefits on both sides, but had anything in the formal curriculum been addressed?

Concerned that it might not have, Nick and Lorraine consulted the Key Stage 1 English Programmes of Study and were surprised to find that, with the exception of presenting their work to an audience, the children had achieved a great deal. All the statements of attainment in the profile component on Talking and Listening had been covered, as had some in the sections on Reading and Writing. They had also touched on areas of mathematics, science and design technology.

Story and the bilingual classroom assistant

> There is a sense of community in the successful multilingual classroom. Linguistic and cultural similarities and differences between children are central to the learning that goes on there ... I do believe that children are empowered if that which is shared and common, as well as that which is personal and individual, has status in the classroom.
> (Savva 1990)

In many multi-ethnic schools, the creation of Savva's 'successful multilingual classroom' is the result of well-planned and thoughtful collaboration between bilingual classroom assistants and class teachers. The role of the bilingual assistant, established through Section 11 funding (now EMAG), has enabled schools and Multicultural Education Services to utilise the linguistic expertise of local minority ethnic communities by employing highly resourceful people, usually women. With their bilingualism as a medium for learning, the presence in the classroom of an adult bilingual person not only helps to raise the status of minority ethnic languages, it encourages both bilingual and monolingual children to appreciate the immense variety of language.

In the case of picture story books, even when the language of the text and the words of the storyteller are seemingly incomprehensible, the child uses their knowledge of narrative to read the signals conveyed through illustrations and thereby construct hypotheses about such things as atmosphere and emotion (Bromley 1996). Sharing stories in other languages encourages speculation about text and an 'ear' for repetition

(NATE 1998). It sharpens the use of wider reading strategies that the child can then apply more consciously to texts in their own or their dominant language. However, the use of bilingual story needs to be part of a broader raft of strategies and texts need to be assessed for their suitability. Gravelle (1998) makes a number of points concerning the selection and use of dual language stories which need to be borne in mind:

- bilingual stories should be readily accessible to pupils;
- they should reflect the nature of modern Britain;
- they should reflect the culture of the language in which they are written.

Gravelle makes the point, also brought to our attention by the bilingual assistants with whom we have worked, that the quality of translation can be variable. The incorrect translation of a single word can change the context and meaning for the child. Before buying dual-language books it is therefore advisable to ask the bilingual assistant to check for any errors.

For those teachers who are bilingual themselves or have opportunities to work with bilingual adults in the classroom, textual errors can be overcome by telling the story rather than reading it. A colleague of mine, Manjula Koria, did just that with the story *The Night the Animals Fought* (Zaton 1988). She used the text and illustrations as a framework for storytelling. By doing so she thought the story would be more spontaneous and would give her greater opportunity to observe pupils' reactions. Bilingual storytelling was a new venture for the school and Manjula used her experience, gained in other schools, to guide the teachers with whom she worked. Before telling the story in Gujarati, Manjula showed the class the cover of the book and asked where the story might be from and what it might be about. This is now a fairly typical procedure within literacy hour and encourages prediction skills by getting pupils to focus on contextual clues. Manjula then explained that she knew several languages and that at home she spoke Gujarati more than she did English. Experience had demonstrated to her that bilingual pupils can be very reticent about admitting their bilingualism. In conversation with me she recalled how as a child her mother had told her it was rude to speak Gujarati in the presence of English people and that she should whisper when in public. By talking in an upbeat way about her own language use she hoped to raise the esteem of the bilingual children sat on the carpet in front of her. After familiarising the pupils with a few Gujarati words to listen out for, Manjula told the story, followed by the English version told by the class teacher. When other teachers heard about the storytelling they were so enthusiastic that Manjula ended up doing the same for every class from Year 1 to Year 7.

In common with other bilingual assistants, interviewed while writing this book, Manjula found that bilingual storytelling had advantages for bilingual and monolingual English speaking pupils alike. Broadly these advantages can be observed as cognitive, motivational and affective responses. For bilingual pupils the cognitive responses included: better understanding of the story, increased knowledge of a topic and more relevant comments about the story because understanding had been enhanced. Bilingual pupils became more involved in listening to the story when it was told bilingually and concentrated more than when stories were told in English. We might describe these responses as motivational ones. Under the third category, affective responses, our colleagues noted the way that during and after such sessions bilingual pupils showed greater self-esteem. In the past, some teachers have been criticised by parents who protested about their children being taught a 'foreign' language. One wonders whether or not those same parents would have had qualms about the story being read in French. They need not have worried. English monolingual pupils seemed to accrue as many, if not more, benefits as their bilingual peers. The bilingual story sessions increased their awareness of languages and culture. It enhanced their use of observational strategies by encouraging the use of visual clues, such as pictures and gestures, to make predictions. There were also suggestions that it made pupils more receptive to learning a second language. During silent reading time some monolingual pupils used the dual language dictionary that had been left in the classroom. Others asked their bilingual classmates what particular objects were called in their language. In addition to the cognitive responses, this latter observation points to the social benefits of bilingual storytelling. The interest generated around language encouraged social interaction outside the classroom, a point noted earlier in the discussion of the effect on pupils of storytelling in the Bushfield project.

What is evident from our experience of bilingual storytelling and storytelling generally is their tremendous social consequence. Storytelling not only stimulates the imagination, it inspires talk. Unlike reading, its dramatic presentation helps to create a social context in which the right to talk is affirmed. Children seem to sense this intuitively and feel empowered to extend the boundaries of oracy into their own lives in order to create and re-create social relationships. Given this point, it would be perilous for teachers to lose sight of the wider usage of language and the power of storytelling in the drive for closer scrutiny of words, sentences and texts. In so many places in the world language and ethnicity have been the basis of a tribalism that has borne tragic consequences. By bringing languages together in a purposeful context for

117

learning through the medium of storytelling, we have seen our colleagues provide the means for children to learn that language is for sharing and that different languages need not be the markers of difference between people and the separateness of their lives. If we can teach this to all our children then we shall have truly raised the standard of educational achievement by preparing 'pupils for the opportunities, responsibilities and experiences ...' of life in a dynamic multicultural society.

References

Apple, M. W. (1986) *Teachers and Texts: a Political Economy of Class and Gender Relations in Education*. London: Routledge and Kegan Paul.

Bromley, H. (1996) '"Madam! Read the scary book, Madam": Momahl and her picture books – the emergent bilingual reader', in Watson, V. and Styles, N. (eds) *Taking Pictures: Pictorial Texts and Young Readers*, 136-44. London: Hodder & Stoughton.

Bullock, Sir Alan (1975) *A Language for Life: Report of the Committee of Inquiry* [in *Reading and the Use of English*] *appointed by the Secretary of State for Education and Science under the Chairmanship of Sir Alan Bullock*. London: HMSO.

Carter, R. (1990) *Knowledge About Language and the Curriculum*. London: Hodder & Stoughton.

Cummins, J. (1984) *Bilingualism and Special Education: Issues in Assessment and Pedagogy*. Clevedon: Multilingual Matters.

DES (1989) *Report of the English Working Party 5-16*. London: HMSO.

DFE (1995) *Key Stages 1 and 2 of the National Curriculum*. London: HMSO.

Gravelle, M. (1998) Dual Language Texts – what do they have to offer? *The Primary English Magazine*. September/October 1998.

Gregory, E. (1996) *Making Sense of a New World: Learning to Read in a Second Language*. London: Paul Chapman Publishing.

Grugeon, E., Hubbard, L., Smith, C. and Dawes, L. (1998) *Teaching Speaking and Listening in the Primary School: Literacy through Oracy*. London: David Fulton.

Halliday, M. A. K. (1978) *Language as Social Semiotic: the Social Interpretation of Language and Meaning*. London: Edward Arnold.

Heath, S. B. (1988) 'What no bedtime story means: narrative skills at home and school', in Mercer, N. (ed.) *Language and Literacy from an Educational Perspective Vol 2*. Milton Keynes: Open University Press.

Hubbard, L. and Hubbard, N. (1989) 'Topiwalo and the National Curriculum. Working with bilingual children', *Early Years Journal of TACTYC* **10** (1), 16-19.

Hymes, D. (1974) *Foundations in Sociolinguistics.* Philadelphia: University of Philadelphia Press.

Jago, M. (1999) 'Bilingual children in a monolingual society', in David, T. (ed.) *Young Children Learning.* London: Paul Chapman Publishing.

NATE (1998) *Position Papers No.3: Literacy.* Sheffield: National Association for the Teaching of English.

Savva, H. (1990) 'The rights of the bilingual child', in Carter, R. (ed.) *Knowledge about Language and the Curriculum*, 248-68. London: Hodder & Stoughton.

SCAA (1996) *Teaching English as an Additional Language: a Framework for Policy.* London: SCAA Publications.

Shuman, R. B. (1978) *Educational Drama for Today's Schools.* Metuchen, New Jersey: Scarecrow Press.

Topiwalo the Hatmaker (undated). Stanmore: Harmony.

Trudgill, P. (1983) *Sociolinguistics: an introduction to language and society.* London: Penguin.

Vygotsky, L (1986) *Thought and Language,* (revised edition by Kozulin, A.) London: MIT Press.

Way, B. (1967) *Development through Drama.* London: Longman.

Woods, P. (1995) *Creative Teachers in Primary Schools.* Buckingham: Open University Press.

Zaton, J. (1988) *The Night the Animals Fought.* London: Mantra Publishing.

Postscript

As a result of our work in the classroom over many years we have come to feel and understand the power of storytelling. Throughout the book we have discussed the numerous functions of story and those who tell stories. During periods of rapid educational change teachers have to meet many challenges and adapt to new ways of working, with fresh orientations in the curriculum. Pressures on teachers from external sources may cause doubt about our methods. While there is always a case to be made for developing new and effective ways of teaching and learning, there is a danger that we may discard what has already proven to be effective. We have made a case for retaining story as one strategy at the heart of primary practice. As advocates of story we have recognised the importance of traditional tales and of teachers having a repertoire of stories they are able to tell with the full dramatic force of the oral tradition. We have also strongly recommended that such a repertoire includes stories which reflect and reveal the multi-lingual and multi-cultural reality of modern Britain.

It seems fitting, therefore, to end the book with a story which can be added to the reader's growing collection. In its retelling, through the medium of a different voice, it will take on new resonances – but that is the nature of the oral tradition.

Hi, hello, Buongiorno

Angela shivered as she walked to school. She left the house in a rush and had foolishly forgotten her coat. Just as she was about to turn back to get it she met her friend, Reshma.

'Hi, Angela,' called Reshma.

'Hello,' replied Angela.

'You look cold.'

'I'm freezing,' stammered Angela.

'Where's your coat?' Reshma asked.

' I was in too much of a hurry. Overslept,' replied Angela.

'Well, you can have my tracksuit top. I won't need it 'til Games,' said Reshma as she opened her school bag.

'Thanks, that's better,' said Angela, relieved as the warmth began to spread through her body.

Angela and Reshma walked to school chatting. As they got close to their friend Gina's house, Gina came rushing down her garden path.

'Hello Gina,' they both said.

'Buongiorno,' Gina replied.

Angela and Reshma looked at one another, puzzled.

'Did I just say buongiorno?' Gina asked, giving a little giggle.

'Yeah,' replied her two bemused friends.

'What does it mean?' enquired Angela.

'It means hello. I've just been speaking Italian with my mum and forgot to change to English. Come on, or we'll be late for school.'

Ms Cohen, their class teacher, was already in class, greeting the children as they entered. She always greeted her pupils in the same way. *'Hello, and how are you today?'* Gina whispered something to her two friends.

'Hello, girls, and how are you today?' Said Ms Cohen cheerily.

'Buongiorno,' returned Gina, Angela and Reshma, simultaneously.

Ms Cohen immediately stopped writing on the board. For a split second she looked surprised and then said, 'Buongiorno. Come sta?'

Reshma and Angela stopped giggling; Gina looked surprised. 'Bene, grazie,' she replied after a pause and then said, 'When did you learn Italian, Ms Cohen?'

'I went on holiday to Italy last year. Every year I go to a different country but before I go I always make an effort to learn some of the language. Then I can make myself understood.'

The next day on their way to school, Reshma taught her two friends a new greeting.

Ms Cohen saw the girls approaching the classroom. 'Buongiorno,' she called.

'Assalum alleykum,' they replied, giggling.

'Valeykum, assalaam. Aap kaisse hey?' replied Ms Cohen.

Angela and Gina stopped giggling. Reshma looked surprised. 'Me teek hu,' she replied after a pause and then said, 'When did you learn Urdu, Ms Cohen?'

'When I moved house. My new neighbours are Muslim. The little girl next door taught me,' answered the teacher.

Finding different ways to say 'hello' to Ms Cohen became quite a game for the three friends. They wanted to be able to catch her out but every time they found a new greeting, their teacher already knew the language and could answer them back. At playtimes they asked their other friends if they knew more ways of saying 'hello'.

Robert said, 'watchyer,' Darren said 'alright?' and Samantha put on a very haughty voice when she said, 'good to see you'. But the girls were looking for something different. Soon, almost half the children in the playground were asking one another how they greeted their friends. Then Rupinder came running up to them, shouting excitedly,' Sat Sri Akal, Sat Sri Akal'.

'What do we say?' asked Angela.

'You say, "Sat Sri Akal", back,' replied Rupinder. 'It's Punjabi'.

The next day, the three girls entered the classroom wearing broad, self-satisfied smiles. They were about to greet Ms Cohen with their new greeting when she spoke first.

'Shalom'.

The smiles drained from the faces of the three girls. They looked at one another and shrugged.

'Okay, Ms Cohen you win,' sighed Angela.

'It's Hebrew,' said the teacher. 'When I meet my family, we say shalom.'

'What do we say in reply,' asked Gina.

'You say shalom, too,' answered Ms. Cohen.

'It's like sat sri akal, Ms,' said Reshma. 'That's what we were going to say to you.'

'Which language is that?'

'You mean, you don't know Ms. We thought you knew all the languages. We could have caught you out. It's Panjabi,' replied Reshma, exasperated.

'I didn't know that,' returned the teacher. She looked at Rupinder and gave a very quick wink.

'Ms Cohen, why are there so many different greetings and what do they all mean,' enquired Angela.

'Well, shalom means 'peace'. Each language has its own way of saying hello. Even among people who speak the same language there are different ways of greeting one another.

How could we find out what all the greetings mean?'

'We could ask the people who say them,' suggested Angela. Then, turning to Reshma, 'what does Assalum alleykum mean?'

'I don't know, but my mum will. I'll ask her tonight.'

'Angela, what does hello mean?' Asked Ms Cohen.

'Well, it's just hello, Ms.'

'Why don't you three try to find out the meanings of all the greetings you've discovered,' suggested Ms Cohen. 'Then you can tell the rest of us.'

'I'd like that,' said Angela.

'Me too,' added Gina.

'Ye atcha khayal hay,' said Reshma, and with a giggle added, 'That's a good idea.'

Index